P9-CBY-896

Birds of Maine
Field Guide

by Stan Tekiela

ADVENTURE PUBLICATIONS
CAMBRIDGE, MINNESOTA

To my wife, Katherine, and daughter, Abigail, with all my love

ACKNOWLEDGMENTS:

Special thanks to Peter Vickery, Ph.D., Department of Natural Resources Conservation, University of Massachusetts, for reviewing the range maps.

Edited by Sandy Livoti

Range maps produced by Anthony Hertzel

Cover and book design and illustrations by Jonathan Norberg

Photo credits by photographer and page number:

Cover photo: Northern Cardinal by Stan Tekiela
Brian M. Collins: 178, 240, 248 **Cornell Laboratory of Ornithology**: 68 (female), 212 (both) **Dudley Edmondson**: 16, 18 (soaring), 50 (soaring), 54 (all), 78, 80, 88, 92 (both), 116, 122 (in flight), 130 (both), 132 (male), 142 (displaying), 148 (female), 152 (soaring), 166 (both), 172 (male), 192 (male), 202, 208, 210 (male), 216 (perching, soaring), 218, 220 (winter, displaying), 258 (in flight), 262 (breeding), 264 (breeding), 268 (male, winter male), 270, 274 (male), 284 **Carrol Henderson**: 86 **Mike Hopiak/Cornell Laboratory of Ornithology**: 70 (perching) **Isidor Jeklin/Cornell Laboratory of Ornithology**: 66 **Kevin T. Karlson**: 38, 144 (both), 172 (female), 260 (winter), 276 (female), 278 **Bruce Leventhal**: 266 **Bill Marchel**: 24 (male), 26, 68 (male), 84, 96 (white-striped), 102, 128, 152 (perching), 162, 192 (female), 228, 230 (both), 236, 242, 246, 254 **Maslowski Wildlife Productions**: 22 (female), 70 (soaring), 74, 100, 104, 112, 118 (female), 124, 182, 184, 200, 250 (male), 272, 282 **Steve Mortensen**: 24 (female), 28 (male), 30 (both), 44 (both), 46, 50 (perching), 58, 60, 62 (both), 94, 158, 164, 196, 214, 232, 268 (female), 286 (both) **Warren Nelson**: 28 (female), 132 (female), 274 (female) **John Pennoyer**: 82, 238, 244 (male) **Brian E. Small**: 36, 40, 114 (winter), 138, 142 (breeding), 148 (male), 150, 156, 244 (yellow male), 256 (in flight), 260 (breeding), 262 (winter, juvenile), 264 (winter), 276 (male) **Stan Tekiela**: 2, 4, 6 (both), 8, 10, 12, 14, 20, 22 (male), 32 (breeding), 34, 42, 48, 52 (both), 56, 64 (both), 72, 76 (both), 90, 96 (tan-striped), 98 (both), 106, 108 (adult, 1 year old), 110, 114 (breeding), 118 (juvenile), 120, 122 (perching), 126, 134, 136 (both), 140, 146 (both), 160, 168, 170, 174, 176 (soaring), 180 (all), 186, 188, 190, 194, 198, 204, 206, 210 (female), 216 (juvenile), 224 (both), 226, 234, 252, 256 (perching, juvenile), 258 (perching), 288 **Brian K. Wheeler**: 18 (perching), 154 (both), 176 (perching), 222 (all) **Jim Zipp**: 32 (winter), 108 (Bohemian), 280

To the best of the publisher's knowledge, all photos except the female Indigo Bunting were of live birds.

20 19 18 17 16 15 14 13

Birds of Maine Field Guide
Copyright © 2002 by Stan Tekiela
Published by Adventure Publications
An imprint of AdventureKEEN
310 Garfield Street South
Cambridge, Minnesota 55008
(800) 678-7006
www.adventurepublications.net
All rights reserved
Printed in China
ISBN 978-1-885061-46-1 (pbk.)

TABLE OF CONTENTS

Introduction

WHY WATCH BIRDS IN MAINE?

Millions of people have discovered bird feeding. It's a simple and enjoyable way to bring the beauty of birds closer to your home. Watching birds at your feeder often leads to a lifetime pursuit of bird identification. The *Birds of Maine Field Guide* is for those who want to identify the common birds of Maine.

There are over 1,100 species of birds found in North America. In Maine alone there have been more than 415 different kinds of birds recorded throughout the years. These bird sightings were diligently recorded by hundreds of bird watchers and became part of the official state record. From these valuable records, I've chosen 119 of the most common birds of Maine to include in this field guide.

Bird watching, often called birding, is one of the most popular activities in America. Its outstanding appeal in Maine is due, in part, to an unusually rich and abundant birdlife. Why are there so many birds? One reason is open space. Maine is over 33,000 square miles (85,800 sq. km), making it the thirty-ninth largest state. Maine is the largest of New England states, having an area that is nearly equal to all other New England states combined. Despite its large size, only about 1.2 million people call Maine home. On average, that's only 41 people per square mile (16 per sq. km). Most of these people are located in and around only three major cities.

Open space is not the only reason there is such an abundance of birds. It's also the diversity of habitat. The state can be divided into three main regions—the Seaboard Lowland, New England Upland and White Mountains.

The Seaboard Lowland is a coastal border that is 30 to 60 miles (48 to 97 km) wide. This is a region with pine-covered, gently rolling hills and isolated rock outcroppings. It is also an area where fresh water flows out of the land from rivers and mixes with saltwater from the ocean, creating a rich habitat known as an estuary. This habitat supports a very diverse bird population that includes Ring-billed Gulls, Ospreys and many shorebird species such as Spotted Sandpipers.

Maine has 228 miles (367 km) of coastline. Including the bays, inlets, river estuaries and islands, there is more than 3,000 miles (4,830 km) of coastal surface. These coastal areas are home to many ocean-loving birds such as the colony-nesting Common Tern, Arctic Tern and Ruddy Turnstone. Maine also has many freshwater and saltwater marshes. The marshes are great places to see water birds such as Great Blue Herons.

Inland from the coastal plain is a region called the New England Upland. The rolling topography here is covered with forests and dotted with clear lakes and rivers. This region offers habitat for Wood Ducks, Ring-necked Ducks and other waterfowl. It is a great place to see an altogether different group of birds than those found in the Seaboard Lowland.

The White Mountains in the western portion of the state add to the great diversity of birds in Maine. This mountainous habitat is entirely different from habitats seen elsewhere in the state. Birds that are more characteristic of the northern forest, such as the Red-breasted Nuthatch and Dark-eyed Junco, are found here.

Finally, varying weather in Maine attracts many different birds. High elevations in the western part of the state are much colder and snowier than habitats near the ocean. Winter temperatures across Maine stay below freezing during winter, while summers can be hot and humid.

Whether watching a nesting colony of herons and egrets near the Atlantic Ocean or welcoming back the hummingbirds in spring, bird watchers enjoy variety and excitement in the birds of Maine as each season turns to the next.

OBSERVE WITH A STRATEGY;
TIPS FOR IDENTIFYING BIRDS

Identifying birds isn't as difficult as you might think. By simply following a few basic strategies, you can increase your chances of successfully identifying most birds you see! One of the first and easiest things to do when you see a new bird is to note its color. (Also, since this book is organized by color, you will go right to that color section to find it.)

Next, note the size of the bird. A strategy to quickly estimate size is to select a small-, medium- and large-sized bird to use for reference. For example, most people are familiar with robins. A robin, measured from tip of the bill to tip of the tail, is 10 inches (25 cm) long. Using the robin as an example of a medium-sized bird, select two other birds, one smaller and one larger. Many people use a House Sparrow, at about 6 inches (15 cm), and an American Crow, about 18 inches (45 cm). When you see a bird that you don't know, you can quickly ask yourself, "Is it smaller than a robin, but larger than a sparrow?" When you look in your field guide to help identify your bird, you'll know it's roughly between 6 and 10 inches (15 to 25 cm) long. This will help to narrow your choices.

Next, note the size, shape and color of the bill. Is it long, short, thick, thin, pointed, blunt, curved or straight? Seed-eating birds, such as Northern Cardinals, have bills that are thick and strong enough to crack even the toughest seeds. Birds that sip nectar, such as Ruby-throated Hummingbirds, need long thin bills to reach deep into flowers. Hawks and owls tear their prey with very sharp, curving bills. Sometimes, just noting the bill shape can help you decide if the bird is a woodpecker, finch, grosbeak, blackbird or bird of prey.

Next, take a look around and note the habitat in which you see the bird. Is it wading in a saltwater marsh? Walking along a riverbank or on the beach? Soaring in the sky? Is it perched high in the trees or hopping along the forest floor? Because of their preferences in diet and habitat, you'll usually see robins hopping on the ground, but not often eating seeds at a feeder. Or you will see a Blue Jay sitting on the branches of a tree, but not climbing headfirst down a tree trunk like the White-breasted Nuthatch.

Noticing what a bird is eating will give you another clue to help you identify that bird. Feeding is a big part of any bird's life. Fully one-third of all bird activity revolves around searching for and catching food, or actually eating. While birds don't always follow all the rules of what we think they eat, you can make some general assumptions. Northern Flickers, for instance, feed upon ants and other insects, so you wouldn't expect to see them visiting a backyard feeder. Some birds, such as Barn Swallows and Tree Swallows, feed upon flying insects, and spend hours swooping and diving to catch a meal.

Sometimes you can identify a bird by the way it perches. Body posture can help you differentiate between an American Crow and a Red-tailed Hawk. American Crows lean forward over their feet on a branch, while hawks perch in a vertical position. Look for this the next time you see a large unidentified bird in a tree.

Birds in flight are often difficult to identify, but noting the size and shape of the wing will help. A bird's wing size is in direct proportion to its body size, weight and type of flying. The shape of the wing determines if the bird flies fast and with precision, or slowly and less precisely. Birds such as House Finches, which flit around in thick tangles of branches, have short round wings. Birds that soar on warm updrafts of air, such as Turkey Vultures, have long broad wings. Barn Swallows have short pointed wings that slice through air, propelling their swift and accurate flight.

Some birds have unique flight patterns that aid in identification. American Goldfinches fly in a distinctive up-and-down pattern that makes it look as if they are riding a roller coaster.

While it's not easy to make these observations in the short time you often have to watch a "mystery bird," practicing these methods of identification will greatly expand your skills in birding. Also, seek the guidance of a more experienced birder who will help you improve your skills and answer questions on the spot.

BIRD BASICS

It's easier to identify birds and communicate about them if you know the names of the different parts of a bird. For instance, it's more effective to use the word "crest" to indicate the set of extra long feathers on top of a Northern Cardinal's head than to try to describe it.

The following illustration points out the basic parts of a bird. Because it is a composite of many birds, it shouldn't be confused with any actual bird.

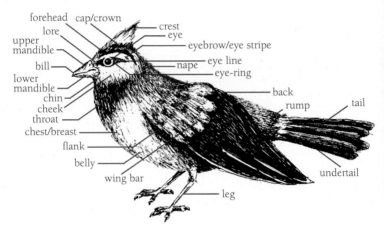

BIRD COLOR VARIABLES

No other animal has a color palette like a bird's. Brilliant blues, lemon yellows, showy reds and iridescent greens are commonplace within the bird world. In general, the male birds are more colorful than their female counterparts. This is probably to help the male attract a mate, essentially saying, "Hey, look at me!" It also calls attention to the male's overall health. The better the condition of his feathers, the better his food source and territory, and therefore the better his potential for a mate.

Female birds that don't look like their male counterparts (such species are called sexually dimorphic, meaning "two forms") are often a nondescript color, as seen with Rose-breasted Grosbeaks. These muted tones help to hide the females during weeks of motionless incubation, and draw less attention to them when they are out feeding or taking a break from the rigors of raising their young.

In some species, such as the Bald Eagle, Blue Jay and Downy Woodpecker, the male birds look nearly identical to the females. In the case of the woodpeckers, the sexes are only differentiated by a single red or sometimes yellow mark. Depending on the species, the mark may be on top of the head, face, nape of the neck or just behind the bill.

During the first year, juvenile birds often look like the mothers. Since brightly colored feathers are used mainly for attracting a mate, young non-breeding males don't have a need for colorful plumage. It is not until the first spring molt (or several years later, depending on the species) that young males obtain their breeding colors.

Both breeding and winter plumages are the result of molting. Molting is the process of dropping old worn feathers and replacing them with new ones. All birds molt, typically twice a year, with the spring molt usually occurring in late winter. During this time, most birds produce their breeding plumage (brighter colors for attracting mates), which lasts throughout the summer.

Winter plumage is the result of the late summer molt, which serves a couple of important functions. First, it adds feathers for warmth in the coming winter. Second, in some species it produces feathers that tend to be drab in color, which helps to camouflage the birds and hide them from predators. The winter plumage of the male American Goldfinch, for example, is an olive brown, unlike its obvious canary yellow color in summer. Luckily for us, some birds, such as the male Northern Cardinal, retain their bright summer colors all year long.

Bird Nests

Bird nests are truly an amazing feat of engineering. Imagine building your home strong enough to weather a storm, large enough to hold your entire family, insulated enough to shelter them from cold and heat, and waterproof enough to keep out rain. Now, build it without any blueprints or directions, and without the use of your hands or feet! Birds do!

Before building a nest, an appropriate site must be selected. In some species, such as House Wrens, the male picks out several potential sites and assembles several small twigs in each. This discourages other birds from using nearby nest cavities. These "extra" nests are occasionally called dummy nests. The female is then taken around and shown all the choices. She chooses her favorite and finishes constructing the nest. In some other species of birds–Baltimore Orioles, for example–it is the female who chooses the site and builds the nest with the male offering only an occasional suggestion. Each species has its own nest-building routine, which is strictly followed.

Nesting material usually consists of natural elements found in the immediate area. Most nests consist of plant fibers (such as bark peeled from grapevines), sticks, mud, dried grass, feathers, fur, or soft fuzzy tufts from thistle. Some birds, including Ruby-throated Hummingbirds, use spider webs to glue nest materials together. Nesting material is limited to what a bird can hold or carry. Because of this, a bird must make many trips afield to gather enough materials to complete its nest. Most nests take at least four days or more, and hundreds, if not thousands, of trips to build.

As you'll see in the following illustrations, birds build a wide variety of nest types.

| ground nest | platform nest | cup nest | pendulous nest | cavity nest |

The simple **ground nest** is scraped out of the earth. A shallow depression that usually contains no nesting material, it is made by birds such as the Killdeer and Horned Lark.

Another kind of nest, the **platform nest**, represents a more complex type of nest building. Constructed of small twigs and branches, the platform nest is a simple arrangement of sticks which forms a platform and features a small depression to nestle the eggs.

Some platform nests, such as those of the Common Loon, are constructed on the ground and are made of mud and grass. Platform nests can also be on cliffs, bridges, balconies or even in flowerpots. This kind of nest gives space to adventurous young-sters and functions as a landing platform for the parents. Many waterfowl construct platform nests on the ground, usually near water or actually in the water. These floating platform nests vary with the water level, thus preventing nests with eggs from being flooded. Platform nests, constructed by such birds as Mourning Doves and herons, are not anchored to the tree and may tumble from the branches during high winds and storms.

The **cup nest** is a modified platform nest, used by three-quarters of all songbirds. Constructed from the outside in, a supporting platform is constructed first. This platform is attached firmly to a tree, shrub, rock ledge or the ground. Next, the sides are con-structed of grasses, small twigs, bark or leaves, which are woven together and often glued with mud for additional strength. The inner cup, lined with feathers, animal fur, soft plant material or animal hair, is constructed last. The mother bird uses her chest to cast the final contours of the inner nest.

The **pendulous nest** is an unusual nest, looking more like a sock hanging from a branch than a nest. Inaccessible to most predators, these nests are attached to the ends of the smallest branches of a tree, and often wave wildly in the breeze. Woven very tightly of plant fibers, they are strong and watertight, taking up to a week to build. More commonly used by tropical birds, this complicated nest type has also been mastered by orioles and kinglets. A small opening on the top or side allows the parents access to the grass-lined interior. (It must be one heck of a ride to be inside one of these nests during a windy spring thunderstorm!)

Another type of nest, the **cavity nest**, is used by many birds, including woodpeckers and Eastern Bluebirds. The cavity nest is usually excavated in a tree branch or trunk and offers shelter from storms, sun, predators and cold. A relatively small entrance hole in a tree leads to an inner chamber up to 10 inches (25 cm) below. Usually constructed by woodpeckers, the cavity nest is typically used only once by its builder, but subsequently can be used for many years by birds such as Wood Ducks, mergansers and bluebirds, which do not have the capability of excavating one for themselves. Kingfishers, on the other hand, excavate a tunnel up to 4 feet (1 m) long, which connects the entrance in a riverbank to the nest chamber. These cavity nests are often sparsely lined because they are already well insulated.

One of the most clever of all nest types is known as the **no nest** or daycare nest. Parasitic birds, such as Brown-headed Cowbirds, build no nests at all! The egg-laden female expertly searches out other birds' nests and sneaks in to lay one of her own eggs while the host mother is not looking, thereby leaving the host mother to raise an adopted youngster. The mother cowbird wastes no energy building a nest only to have it raided by a predator. By using several nests of other birds, she spreads out her progeny so at least one of her offspring will live to maturity.

Some birds, including some swallows, take nest building one step further. They use a collection of small balls of mud to construct an adobe-style home. Constructed beneath the eaves of houses, under bridges or inside chimneys, some of these nests look like simple cup nests. Others are completely enclosed, with small tunnel-like openings that lead into a safe nesting chamber for the baby birds.

WHO BUILDS THE NEST?

In general, the female bird builds the nest. She gathers nesting materials and constructs a nest, with an occasional visit from her mate to check on the progress. In some species, both parents contribute equally to the construction of a nest. A male bird might forage for precisely the right sticks, grass or mud, but it's often the female that forms or puts together the nest. She uses her body to form the egg chamber. Rarely does the male build a nest by himself.

FLEDGING

Fledging is the interval between hatching and flight or leaving the nest. Some birds leave the nest within hours of hatching (precocial), but it might be weeks before they are able to fly. This is common with waterfowl and shorebirds. Until they start to fly, they are called fledglings. Birds that are still in the nest are called nestlings. Other baby birds are born naked and blind, and remain in the nest for several weeks (altricial).

WHY BIRDS MIGRATE

Why do birds migrate? The short answer is simple–food. Birds migrate to areas with high concentrations of food, as it is easier to breed where food is than where it is not. A typical migrating bird–the Rose-breasted Grosbeak, for instance–migrates from the tropics of Central and South America to nest in the forests of North America, taking advantage of billions of newly hatched insects to feed its young. This trip is called **complete migration**.

Other migrators, such as some birds of prey, migrate back to northern regions in spring. In these locations, they hunt mice, voles and other small rodents, which are beginning to breed.

Complete migrators have a set time and pattern of migration. Each year at nearly the same time, they take off and head for a specific wintering ground. Complete migrators may travel great distances, sometimes as much as 15,000 miles (24,150 km) or more in a year. But complete migration doesn't necessarily imply flying from the cold, frozen northland to a tropical destination. The Dark-eyed Junco, for example, is a complete migrator that flies from the far reaches of Canada to spend the winter right here in Maine.

There are many interesting aspects to complete migrators. In the spring, males usually migrate several weeks before the females, arriving early to scope out possibilities for nesting sites and food sources, and to begin to defend territories. The females arrive several weeks later. In the autumn, in many species, the females and their young leave early, often up to four weeks before the adult males.

All migrators are not the same type. There are **partial migrators**, such as American Goldfinches, that usually wait until the food supply dwindles before flying south. Unlike complete migrators, the partial migrators move only far enough south, or sometimes east and west, to find abundant food. In some years it might be only a few hundred miles, while in other years it might be nearly a thousand. This kind of migration, dependent on the weather and available food, is sometimes called **seasonal movement**.

Unlike the predictable ebbing and flowing behavior of complete migrators or partial migrators, **irruptive migrators** can move every third to fifth year or, in some cases, in consecutive years. These migrations are triggered when times are really tough and food is scarce. Red-breasted Nuthatches are a good example of irruptive migrators, because they leave their normal northern range in search of food or in response to overpopulation.

How Do Birds Migrate?

One of the many secrets of migration is fat. While we humans are fighting the battle of the bulge, birds intentionally gorge themselves to put on as much fat as possible while still being able to fly. Fat provides the greatest amount of energy per unit of weight, and in the same way that your car needs gas, birds are propelled by fat and stalled without it.

During long migratory flights, fat deposits are used up quickly, and birds need to stop to "refuel." This is when backyard bird feeding stations and undeveloped, natural spaces around our towns and cities are especially important. Some birds require up to two to three days of constant feeding to build up their fat reserves before continuing their seasonal trip.

Some birds, such as most eagles, hawks, ospreys, falcons and vultures, migrate during the day. Larger birds can hold more body fat, go longer without eating and take longer to migrate. These birds glide along on rising columns of warm air, called thermals, which hold them aloft while they slowly make their way north or south. They generally rest at night and hunt early in the morning before the sun has a chance to warm up the land and create good soaring conditions. Birds migrating during the day use a combination of landforms, rivers, and the rising and setting sun to guide them in the right direction.

Most other birds migrate during the night. Studies show that some birds which migrate at night use the stars to navigate. Others use the setting sun, while still others, such as doves, use the planet's magnetic field to guide them north or south. While flying at night might seem like a crazy idea, nocturnal migration is safer for several reasons. First, there are fewer nighttime predators for migrating birds. Second, traveling at night allows time during the day to find food in unfamiliar surroundings. Finally, nighttime wind patterns tend to be flat, or laminar. These flat winds don't have the turbulence associated with the daytime winds, and can actually help carry smaller birds by pushing them along.

HOW TO USE THIS GUIDE

To help you quickly and easily identify birds, this book is organized by color. Simply note the color of the bird and turn to that section. Refer to the first page for the color key. The Pileated Woodpecker, for example, is black and white with a red crest. Because the bird is mostly black and white, it will be found in the black and white section. Each color section is also arranged by size, generally with the smaller birds first. Sections may also incorporate the average size in a range, which, in some cases, reflects size differences between the male and female birds. Flip through the pages in that color section to find the bird. If you already know the name of the bird, check the index for the page number. In some species, the male and female are remarkably different in color. In others, the color of the breeding and winter plumages differs. These species have an inset photograph with a page reference and in most cases are found in two color sections.

In the description section you will find a variety of information about the bird. On the next page is a sample of the information included in the book.

RANGE MAPS

Range maps are included for each bird. Colored areas indicate where in Maine a particular bird is most likely to be found. The colors represent the presence of a species during a specific season, not the density or amount of birds in the area. Green is used for summer, blue for winter, red for year-round and yellow for areas where the bird is seen during migration. While every effort has been made to accurately depict these ranges, they are only general guidelines. Ranges actually change on an ongoing basis due to a variety of factors. Changes in the weather, species abundance, landscape and vital resources such as the availability of food and water can affect local populations, migration and movements, causing birds to be found in areas that are atypical for the species.

Colored areas simply mean bird sightings for that species have been frequent in those areas and less frequent in the others. Please use the maps as intended–as general guides only.

COMMON NAME
Scientific name

YEAR-ROUND
MIGRATION
SUMMER
WINTER

Size: measures head to tail, may include wingspan

Male: a brief description of the male bird, and may include breeding, winter or other plumages

Female: a brief description of the female bird, which is sometimes not the same as the male

Juvenile: a brief description of the juvenile bird, which often looks like the female

Nest: the kind of nest this bird builds to raise its young; who builds the nest; how many broods per year

Eggs: how many eggs you might expect to see in a nest; color and marking

Incubation: the average time parents spend incubating the eggs; who does the incubation

Fledging: the average time young spend in the nest after hatching but before they leave the nest; who does the most "childcare" and feeding

Migration: complete (consistent, seasonal), partial migrator (seasonal, destination varies), irruptive (unpredictable, depends on the food supply), non-migrator; additional comments

Food: what the bird eats most of the time (e.g., seeds, insects, fruit, nectar, small mammals, fish); if it typically comes to a bird feeding station

Compare: notes about other birds that look similar, and the pages on which they can be found

Stan's Notes: Interesting gee-whiz natural history information. This could be something to look or listen for, or something to help positively identify the bird. Also includes remarkable features.

female
pg. 105

male

EASTERN TOWHEE
Pipilo erythrophthalmus

SUMMER

Size: 7-8" (18-20 cm)

Male: A mostly black bird with dirty red-brown sides and white belly. Long black tail with white tip. Short, stout, pointed bill and rich red eyes. White wing patches flash in flight.

Female: similar to male, but is brown, not black

Juvenile: light brown, a heavily streaked head, chest and belly, long dark tail with white tip

Nest: cup; female builds; 2 broods per year

Eggs: 3-4; creamy white with brown markings

Incubation: 12-13 days; female incubates

Fledging: 10-12 days; male and female feed young

Migration: complete, southern states, South America

Food: insects, seeds, fruit; visits ground feeders

Compare: Slightly smaller than the American Robin (pg. 211). The Gray Catbird (pg. 205) lacks a black "hood" and rusty sides. Common Grackle (pg. 13) lacks white belly and has long thin bill. Male Rose-breasted Grosbeak (pg. 27) has a rosy patch in center of chest.

Stan's Notes: Common name comes from its distinctive "tow-hee" call given by both sexes. Mostly known for its characteristic call that sounds like, "Drink-your-tea!" Seen hopping backward with both feet (bilateral scratching), raking up leaf litter in search of insects and seeds. The female broods, but the male does the most feeding of young. White-eyed form in southern states, red-eyed elsewhere.

3

female
pg. 111

male

BROWN-HEADED COWBIRD
Molothrus ater

MIGRATION SUMMER

Size: 7½" (19 cm)

Male: A glossy black bird, reminiscent of a Red-winged Blackbird. Chocolate brown head with a pointed, sharp gray bill.

Female: dull brown bird with bill similar to male

Juvenile: similar to female, only dull gray color and a streaked chest

Nest: no nest; lays eggs in nests of other birds

Eggs: 5-7; white with brown markings

Incubation: 10-13 days; host bird incubates eggs

Fledging: 10-11 days; host birds feed young

Migration: complete, to southern states

Food: insects, seeds; will come to seed feeders

Compare: The male Red-winged Blackbird (pg. 9) is slightly larger, with red and yellow patches on upper wings. Common Grackle (pg. 13) has a long tail and lacks the brown head. European Starling (pg. 7) has a shorter tail.

Stan's Notes: A member of the blackbird family. Of more than 100 species of parasitic birds worldwide, this is the only parasitic bird in Maine, laying all eggs in host birds' nests, leaving others to raise its young. Cowbirds are known to have laid eggs in nests of over 200 species of birds. Some birds reject cowbird eggs, but most incubate them and raise the young, even to the exclusion of their own. Look for warblers and other birds feeding young birds twice their own size. At one time cowbirds followed bison to feed on the insects attracted to the animals.

5

winter

breeding

EUROPEAN STARLING
Sturnus vulgaris

Size: 7½" (19 cm)

Male: Gray-to-black bird with white speckles in fall and winter. Shiny purple black during spring and summer. Long, pointed yellow bill in spring turns gray in fall. Short tail.

Female: same as male

Juvenile: similar to adult, gray brown in color with a streaked chest

Nest: cavity; male and female line the cavity; 2 broods per year

Eggs: 4-6; bluish with brown markings

Incubation: 12-14 days; female and male incubate

Fledging: 18-20 days; female and male feed young

Migration: non-migrator to partial migrator; some will move to southern states

Food: insects, seeds, fruit; comes to seed and suet feeders

Compare: Looks similar to Common Grackle (pg. 13), but lacks its long tail.

Stan's Notes: A great songster, this bird can also mimic sounds. Often displaces woodpeckers, chickadees and other cavity-nesting birds. Can be very aggressive and destroy eggs or young of other birds. The bill changes color with the seasons: yellow in spring and gray in autumn. Jaws are designed to be the most powerful when opening, as they pry open crevices to locate hidden insects. Gathers in the hundreds in autumn. Not a native bird, it was introduced to New York City in 1890-91 from Europe.

female pg. 121

male

RED-WINGED BLACKBIRD
Agelaius phoeniceus

SUMMER

Size: 8½" (22 cm)

Male: Jet black bird with red and yellow shoulder patches on upper wings. Pointed black bill.

Female: heavily streaked brown bird with a pointed brown bill and white eyebrows

Juvenile: same as female

Nest: cup; female builds; 2-3 broods per year

Eggs: 3-4; bluish green with brown markings

Incubation: 10-12 days; female incubates

Fledging: 11-14 days; female and male feed young

Migration: complete, to southern states

Food: seeds, insects; will come to seed feeders

Compare: Slightly smaller than male Rusty Blackbird (pg. 11). Slightly larger than male Brown-headed Cowbird (pg. 5), but less iridescent and lacks the brown head of the Cowbird. Differs from all blackbirds due to the red and yellow patches on its wings (epaulets).

Stan's Notes: One of the most widespread and numerous birds in Maine. It's a sure sign of spring when Red-winged Blackbirds return to the marshes. Flocks of up to 10,000 birds have been reported. Males return before females and defend territories by singing from tops of surrounding vegetation. The males repeat call from tops of cattails while showing off their red and yellow shoulder patches. Females choose mate and usually nest over shallow water in thick stands of cattails. Red-wingeds feed mostly on seeds during fall and spring, switching to insects in summer.

female pg. 207

male

RUSTY BLACKBIRD
Euphagus carolinus

MIGRATION
SUMMER

Size: 9" (22.5 cm)

Male: Glossy black in color with highlights of blue and purple. Bright yellow eyes. Has a short, pointed thin bill. Non-breeding plumage is more of a rusty brown than glossy black.

Female: overall gray bird, feathers have rusty edges, eyes yellow, has a short, pointed thin bill, non-breeding is much browner with a gray rump and black patch around each eye

Juvenile: similar to female

Nest: cup; female builds; 1-2 broods per year

Eggs: 4-5; bluish with brown markings

Incubation: 12-14 days; female incubates

Fledging: 11-13 days; male and female feed young

Migration: complete, to southeastern states

Food: insects, seeds

Compare: The male Red-winged Blackbird (pg. 9) is slightly smaller and has red and yellow markings on shoulders. Smaller than the Common Grackle (pg. 13), which has a longer tail.

Stan's Notes: This bird nests across the northern half of Maine in small loose colonies, often preferring more wooded, swampy areas. Male feeds female while she incubates. Gathers in large groups and with other blackbirds to migrate each autumn. When in flight, end of tail often appears squared.

COMMON GRACKLE
Quiscalus quiscula

SUMMER

Size:	11-13" (28-33 cm)
Male:	Large black bird with iridescent blue black head, purple brown body, long black tail, long thin bill and bright golden eyes.
Female:	similar to male, only duller and smaller
Juvenile:	similar to female
Nest:	cup; female builds; 2 broods per year
Eggs:	4-5; greenish white with brown markings
Incubation:	13-14 days; female incubates
Fledging:	16-20 days; female and male feed young
Migration:	complete, to southern states
Food:	fruit, seeds, insects; comes to seed feeders
Compare:	The breeding European Starling (pg. 7) is much smaller, with a speckled appearance and yellow bill. Male Red-winged Blackbird (pg. 9) has red and yellow wing markings. The smaller male Rusty Blackbird (pg. 11) lacks the Grackle's long tail.

Stan's Notes: Usually nests in small colonies of up to 75 pairs, but travels with other blackbirds in large flocks. Is known to feed in farmers' fields. Male holds tail in a deep V shape during flight. The flight pattern is almost always level, as opposed to an undulating up-and-down movement. Unlike most birds, it has larger muscles for opening the mouth (rather than for closing it) and prying crevices apart to locate hidden insects. The name is derived from the Latin word *gracula*, meaning "to croak," for its loud, raspy call.

AMERICAN CROW
Corvus brachyrhynchos

Size: 18" (45 cm)

Male: All-black bird with black bill, legs and feet. Can have a purple sheen in direct sunlight.

Female: same as male

Juvenile: same as adult

Nest: platform; female builds; 1 brood per year

Eggs: 4-6; bluish to olive green, brown markings

Incubation: 18 days; female incubates

Fledging: 28-35 days; female and male feed young

Migration: non-migrator to partial migrator

Food: fruit, insects, mammals, fish, carrion; will come to seed and suet feeders

Compare: Similar to the Common Raven (pg. 17), but has a smaller bill and lacks shaggy throat feathers. Crow has higher-pitched call than the Raven's deep, low raspy call. Crow has a squared tail. Raven has a wedge-shaped tail, apparent in flight.

Stan's Notes: This is one of the most recognizable birds in Maine. Often reuses its nest every year if not taken over by a Great Horned Owl. Collects and stores bright, shiny objects in the nest. Able to mimic other birds and human voices. One of the smartest of all birds and very social, often entertaining itself by provoking chases with other birds. Feeds on roadkill but is rarely hit by cars. Can live up to 20 years. Unmated birds, known as helpers, help raise young. Large extended families roost together at night, dispersing during the day to hunt.

COMMON RAVEN
Corvus corax

YEAR-ROUND

Size: 22-27" (56-69 cm)

Male: Large all-black bird with a large black bill, a shaggy beard of feathers on the chin and throat, and a large wedge-shaped tail, seen in flight.

Female: same as male

Juvenile: same as adult

Nest: platform; female and male build; 1 brood per year

Eggs: 4-6; pale green with brown markings

Incubation: 18-21 days; female incubates

Fledging: 38-44 days; female and male feed young

Migration: non-migrator to partial migrator

Food: insects, fruit, small animals, carrion

Compare: Larger than its cousin, the American Crow (pg. 15), which lacks the throat patch of feathers. Glides on flat outstretched wings, compared to the slightly V-shaped pattern of Crow. Low raspy call distinguishes the Raven from the higher-pitched Crow.

Stan's Notes: Considered by some to be the smartest of all birds. Known for its aerial acrobatics and long swooping dives. Scavenges with crows and gulls. Known to follow wolf packs around to pick up scraps and pick at bones of a kill. Complex courtship includes grabbing bills, preening each other and cooing. Mates are long-term. Uses same nest site for many years. Most don't breed until 3 to 4 years of age.

soaring

TURKEY VULTURE
Cathartes aura

SUMMER

Size: 26-32" (66-80 cm); up to 6-foot wingspan

Male: Large bird with obvious red head and legs. In flight, the wings appear two-toned: black leading edge with gray on the trailing edge and tip. The tips of wings end in finger-like projections. Long squared tail. Ivory bill.

Female: same as male

Juvenile: similar to adult, with gray-to-blackish head and bill

Nest: no nest, or minimal nest on cliff or in cave; 1 brood per year

Eggs: 2; white with brown markings

Incubation: 38-41 days; female and male incubate

Fledging: 66-88 days; female and male feed young

Migration: complete, to southern states, Mexico, and Central and South America

Food: carrion, just about any dead animal of any size; parents regurgitate for young

Compare: Smaller than the Bald Eagle (pg. 55), look for Vulture's two-toned wings. Flies holding wings in a slight V shape, unlike the Eagle's straight wing position.

Stan's Notes: The vulture's naked head is an adaptation to reduce risk of feather fouling (picking up diseases) from carcasses. Unlike hawks and eagles, it has weak feet more suited to walking than grasping. One of the few birds that has a developed sense of smell. Mostly mute, making only grunts and groans. Seen in trees with wings outstretched to catch sun.

drying

DOUBLE-CRESTED CORMORANT
Phalacrocorax auritus

MIGRATION
SUMMER

Size: 33" (84 cm)

Male: Large all-black water bird with long snake-like neck. A long yellow orange bill with a hooked tip.

Female: same as male

Juvenile: lighter brown with a grayish-colored breast and neck

Nest: platform, in colony; male and female build; 1 brood per year

Eggs: 3-4; bluish white without markings

Incubation: 25-29 days; female and male incubate

Fledging: 37-42 days; male and female feed young

Migration: complete, to southern coastal states, Mexico and Central America

Food: small fish, aquatic insects

Compare: Similar size as the Turkey Vulture (pg. 19), which also perches on branches with wings open to dry in sun, but Vulture has a naked red head.

Stan's Notes: Typically flies in a large V-shaped formation. Usually roosts in large colonies in trees close to water. Swims underwater to catch fish, holding its wings at its sides. Lacks the oil gland that keeps feathers from becoming waterlogged. To dry off, it strikes an upright pose with wings outstretched, facing the sun. Gives grunts, pops and groans. Named "Double-crested" for the two crests on its head, which are not often seen. "Cormorant" is a contraction from *corvus marinus*, meaning "crow" or "raven," and "of the sea."

male

female

BLACK-AND-WHITE WARBLER
Mniotilta varia

SUMMER

Size: 5" (13 cm)

Male: Striped like a zebra, this small warbler has a distinctive black-and-white striped cap. White belly. Black chin and cheek patch.

Female: same as male, only duller and without the black chin and cheek patch

Juvenile: similar to female

Nest: cup; female builds; 1 brood per year

Eggs: 4-5; white with brown markings

Incubation: 10-11 days; female incubates

Fledging: 9-12 days; female and male feed young

Migration: complete, to Florida, Mexico, Central and South America

Food: insects

Compare: Look for Warbler to creep down tree trunks headfirst, like the Red-breasted and White-breasted Nuthatches (pp. 187 and 191).

Stan's Notes: The only warbler that moves headfirst down a tree trunk. Look for this common warbler searching for insect eggs in the bark of large trees. Song sounds like a slowly turning, squeaky wheel. Female will perform a distraction dance to draw predators away from the nest. Makes its nest on the ground, concealed under dead leaves or at the base of a tree. A common summer resident, nesting throughout the state. More conspicuous during spring and fall migrations. Most arrive in April to May, and leave by September.

male

female

DOWNY WOODPECKER
Dryobates pubescens

Size: 6" (15 cm)

Male: A small woodpecker with an all-white belly, black-and-white spotted wings, a black line running through the eyes, a short black bill, a white stripe down the back and red mark on the back of the head. Several small black spots along the sides of white tail.

Female: same as male, but lacks a red mark on head

Juvenile: same as female, some have a red mark near the forehead

Nest: cavity; male and female excavate; 1 brood per year

Eggs: 3-5; white without markings

Incubation: 11-12 days; female and male incubate, the female during day, male at night

Fledging: 20-25 days; male and female feed young

Migration: non-migrator

Food: insects, seeds; visits seed and suet feeders

Compare: Almost identical to the Hairy Woodpecker (pg. 31), but smaller. Look for the shorter, thinner bill of Downy to differentiate them.

Stan's Notes: One of the most abundant and widespread woodpeckers in the state, found throughout where trees are present. Stiff tail feathers help brace it like a tripod as it clings to a tree. Like other woodpeckers, it has a long, barbed tongue to pull insects from tiny places. Male and female drum on branches or hollow logs to announce territory, which is rarely larger than 5 acres (2 ha). Male performs most of the brooding. Will winter roost in cavity.

female
pg. 103

male

ROSE-BREASTED GROSBEAK
Pheucticus ludovicianus

SUMMER

Size: 7-8" (18-20 cm)

Male: A plump black-and-white bird with a large, triangular rose patch in the center of chest. Wing linings are rosy red. Large ivory bill.

Female: heavily streaked brown and white bird with large white eyebrows, orange yellow wing linings

Juvenile: same as female

Nest: cup; the female and male build; 1-2 broods per year

Eggs: 3-5; blue green with brown markings

Incubation: 13-14 days; female and male incubate

Fledging: 9-12 days; female and male feed young

Migration: complete, to Mexico, Central America and South America

Food: insects, seeds, fruit; comes to seed feeders

Compare: Male is very distinctive with no look-alikes.

Stan's Notes: Seen across Maine, but is more conspicuous during spring and fall migrations. Often prefers mature deciduous forest for nesting. Both sexes sing, but the male sings much louder and clearer. Has a rich, robin-like song. The name "Grosbeak" refers to its large bill, used to crush seeds. Rose breast patch varies in size and shape in each male. Late to arrive in spring and early to leave in fall. Males arrive in small groups first, joined by females several days later. Several males can be seen visiting seed feeders at the same time during spring. When the females arrive, males become territorial and reduce their visits to feeders. Young grosbeaks visit feeders with adults after fledging.

male

female

YELLOW-BELLIED SAPSUCKER
Sphyrapicus varius

SUMMER

Size: 8-9" (20-22.5 cm)

Male: Medium-sized woodpecker with checkered back. Has a red forehead, crown and chin. Tan-to-yellow breast and belly. White wing patches flash while flying.

Female: similar to male, white chin

Juvenile: similar to female, dull brown and lacks any red marking

Nest: cavity; female and male excavate; 1 brood per year

Eggs: 5-6; white without markings

Incubation: 12-13 days; female and male incubate, the female during day, male at night

Fledging: 25-29 days; female and male feed young

Migration: complete, to southern states, Mexico and Central America

Food: insects, tree sap; comes to suet feeders

Compare: Similar to other woodpeckers, but the male is the only woodpecker in Maine with a red chin. Female has a white chin.

Stan's Notes: Drills holes in a pattern of horizontal rows in small-to medium-sized trees to bleed tree sap. Many birds drink from sapsucker taps. Oozing sap also attracts insects, which sapsuckers eat. Sapsuckers will defend their sapping sites from the other birds. They don't suck sap; rather, they lap it with their long tongues. A quiet bird with few vocalizations, but will mew like a cat. Unlike other woodpeckers, drumming rhythm is irregular.

male

female

YEAR-ROUND

HAIRY WOODPECKER
Dryobates villosus

Size: 9" (22.5 cm)

Male: Black-and-white woodpecker with a white belly, and black wings with rows of white spots. White stripe down back. Long black bill. Red mark on back of head.

Female: same as male, but lacks a red mark on head

Juvenile: grayer version of female

Nest: cavity; female and male excavate; 1 brood per year

Eggs: 3-6; white without markings

Incubation: 11-15 days; female and male incubate, the female during day, male at night

Fledging: 28-30 days; male and female feed young

Migration: non-migrator

Food: insects, nuts, seeds; comes to seed and suet feeders

Compare: Larger than Downy Woodpecker (pg. 25), Hairy has a longer bill and lacks Downy's black spots along tail.

Stan's Notes: A common backyard bird that announces its arrival with a sharp chirp before landing on feeders. Barbed tongue helps extract insects from trees. Responsible for eating many destructive forest insects. Has tiny bristle-like feathers at base of bill to protect the nostrils from wood dust. Will drum on hollow logs, branches or stovepipes in springtime to announce its territory. Often prefers to excavate nest cavities in live aspen trees. Has a larger, more oval-shaped cavity entrance than that of Downy Woodpecker.

winter

breeding

RUDDY TURNSTONE
Arenaria interpres

MIGRATION

Size: 9½" (24 cm)

Male: Breeding has orange legs, a black and white head marking, black bib, white throat and belly, black and chestnut wings and back. Slightly upturned black bill. Winter has a brown and white head and breast pattern.

Female: similar to male, only duller

Juvenile: similar to adults, but black and white head has a scaly appearance

Nest: ground; female builds; 1 brood per year

Eggs: 3-4; olive green with dark markings

Incubation: 22-24 days; male and female incubate

Fledging: 19-21 days; male feeds young

Migration: complete, to southern coastal states, South America

Food: aquatic insects, fish, mollusks, crustaceans, worms, eggs

Compare: Unusually ornamented shorebird. Look for a striking black and white pattern on head and neck, and orange legs to identify.

Stan's Notes: Seen during migration. Also called Rock Plover. Was named "Turnstone" because it turns stones over on rocky beaches to find food. Known for its unusual behavior of robbing and eating other birds' eggs. Hangs around crabbing operations to eat scraps from nets. Can be very tolerant of humans when feeding. Females often leave before the young leave nests (fledge), resulting in the males raising young. Males have a bare spot on the belly (brood patch) to warm the young, something only females normally have.

ATLANTIC PUFFIN
Fratercula arctica

YEAR-ROUND

Size: 12" (30 cm)

Male: Black back with white breast and belly. An oversized orange bill with gray base. White face and dark eyes. Orange legs and feet.

Female: same as male

Juvenile: similar to adult, but gray face with a smaller triangular-shaped bill

Nest: cavity; male digs tunnel under a rock, up to 36 inches (90 cm); 1 brood per year

Eggs: 1; white without markings

Incubation: 39-45 days; male and female incubate

Fledging: 38-44 days; male and female feed young

Migration: partial; moves out to sea for the winter

Food: fish, aquatic insects

Compare: The unique shape and coloring of this bird and its extremely large bill makes it hard to confuse with any other bird.

Stan's Notes: The Atlantic Puffin is one of three puffin species in North America. The other two species, Tufted Puffin and Horned Puffin (not shown), are seen on the West coast. Large colony nester, usually on islands. Male will excavate a tunnel up to three times its own length under a rock, ending in a nest chamber. Nest chamber is lined with grass, leaves and feathers. Adults fly up to 10 miles (16 km) from nest sites and dive down as far as 100 feet (30 m) to catch fish. Young are fed an all-fish diet. Will return to same nest site with same mate each season. Moves off land and out to sea in winter. Formerly known as Common Puffin.

female pg. 139

male

BUFFLEHEAD
Bucephala albeola

MIGRATION
WINTER

Size: 13-15" (33-38 cm)

Male: A small duck with striking white sides and black back. Green purple head with a large white bonnet-like patch.

Female: brown version of male, with a brown head and white patch on cheek, just behind eyes

Juvenile: similar to female

Nest: cavity; female lines old woodpecker cavity; 1 brood per year

Eggs: 8-10; ivory to olive without markings

Incubation: 29-31 days; female incubates

Fledging: 50-55 days; female leads young to food

Migration: complete, along the East coast from Maine to Florida, Mexico and Central America

Food: aquatic insects

Compare: The male Common Goldeneye (pg. 47) is slightly larger, shares the white sides and black back, but lacks the white head patch. Male Hooded Merganser (pg. 43) is similar, but lacks the male Bufflehead's white sides.

Stan's Notes: Common diving duck that travels with other ducks. Usually seen during migration and winter, arriving late in August, wintering in the southern half of Maine. Most commonly found in sheltered bays and coastal harbors, it is also seen inland on rivers and lakes. Nests in old woodpecker cavities. Unlike other ducks, young remain in nests for up to two days before venturing out with their mothers. Female is very territorial and remains with the same mate for many years.

female pg. 151

male

LESSER SCAUP
Aythya affinis

MIGRATION

Size: 16-17" (40-43 cm)

Male: Appears mostly black with bold white sides and gray back. Chest and head look nearly black, but head appears purple with green highlights in direct sun. Bright yellow eyes.

Female: overall brown with dull white patch at base of light gray bill, yellow eyes

Juvenile: same as female

Nest: ground; female builds; 1 brood per year

Eggs: 8-14; olive buff without markings

Incubation: 22-28 days; female incubates

Fledging: 45-50 days; female teaches young to feed

Migration: complete, southern states, Mexico, Central America and northern South America

Food: aquatic plants and insects

Compare: The male Ring-necked Duck (pg. 41) has a bold white ring around its bill and a black back, compared with male Lesser Scaup's gray back. Male Ring-necked lacks the bold white sides of the male Lesser Scaup.

Stan's Notes: Common migrator in Maine. This duck completely submerges itself to feed on the bottom of lakes, unlike dabbling ducks which only tip forward to reach the bottom. Often seen in large flocks on lakes, ponds and sewage lagoons during migration. When seen in flight, note the bold white stripe under the wings. An interesting baby-sitting arrangement in which groups of young are tended by one to three adult females. Prefers fresh water, but can be seen along the coast. Doesn't breed in Maine.

female pg. 157

male

RING-NECKED DUCK
Aythya collaris

MIGRATION
SUMMER

Size: 17" (43 cm)

Male: A striking duck with black head, chest and back. Sides are gray to nearly white. Has a bold white ring around the bill and second ring at base of bill. Top of head is peaked.

Female: dark brown back, light brown sides, a gray face, dark brown crown, white line behind eyes and white ring around the bill, top of head peaked

Juvenile: similar to female

Nest: ground; female builds; 1 brood per year

Eggs: 8-10; olive gray to brown without markings

Incubation: 26-27 days; female incubates

Fledging: 49-56 days; female teaches young to feed

Migration: complete, to southern states, West Indies, Mexico and Central America

Food: aquatic plants and insects

Compare: Similar size as male Lesser Scaup (pg. 39), which has a gray back, compared with the black back of the male Ring-necked Duck. Look for the male Ring-necked's prominent white ring around the bill.

Stan's Notes: A common breeding duck in Maine. Usually is seen in larger freshwater lakes rather than saltwater marshes. A diving duck, watch for it to dive underwater to forage for food. Takes to flight by springing up off water. Named "Ring-necked" because of the cinnamon-colored collar (nearly impossible to see in the field). Also known as Ring-billed Duck due to obvious white ring on bill.

female pg. 161

male

HOODED MERGANSER
Lophodytes cucullatus

YEAR-ROUND
SUMMER

Size: 16-19" (40-48 cm)

Male: A sleek black-and-white bird that has rusty brown sides. Crest "hood" raises to reveal a large white patch. Long, thin black bill.

Female: sleek brown and rust bird with a ragged rusty crest and long, thin brown bill

Juvenile: similar to female

Nest: cavity; female lines old woodpecker hole; 1 brood per year

Eggs: 10-12; white without markings

Incubation: 32-33 days; female incubates

Fledging: 71 days; female feeds young

Migration: complete, to coastal states and Mexico

Food: small fish, aquatic insects

Compare: A distinctive diving bird, look for the male's large white patch on the head and rusty brown sides. Male Bufflehead (pg. 37) is smaller than Hooded Merganser and has white sides. The male Wood Duck (pg. 233) is similar in size, but has a green head.

Stan's Notes: A small diving bird of shallow-water ponds, sloughs, lakes and rivers. It is a summer breeding duck in Maine, rarely seen away from wooded areas, where it nests in natural cavities or nest boxes. Female will "dump" eggs into other Hooded Merganser nests, resulting in 20 to 25 eggs in some nests. Frequently associated with Wood Ducks. Has been known to share a nest cavity with a Wood Duck, sitting side by side. Male Hooded Merganser can voluntarily raise and lower its crest to show off the large white head patch.

male

female

PILEATED WOODPECKER
Dryocopus pileatus

YEAR-ROUND

Size: 19" (48 cm)

Male: Crow-sized woodpecker with a black back and bright red crest. Long gray bill with red mustache. White leading edge of the wings flashes brightly when flying.

Female: same as male, but has a black forehead and lacks red mustache

Juvenile: similar to adults, only duller and browner

Nest: cavity; male and female excavate; 1 brood per year

Eggs: 3-5; white without markings

Incubation: 15-18 days; female and male incubate, the female during day, male at night

Fledging: 26-28 days; female and male feed young

Migration: non-migrator

Food: insects; will come to suet feeders

Compare: This bird is quite distinctive and unlikely to be confused with any others. Look for the Pileated Woodpecker's bright red crest and exceptionally large size.

Stan's Notes: Our largest woodpecker. The common name comes from the Latin *pileatus*, which means "wearing a cap," referring to its crest. Relatively shy bird that prefers large tracts of woodland. Drums on hollow branches, chimneys, etc., to announce territory. Excavates oval holes up to several feet long in tree trunks, looking for insects to eat. Large chips of wood lay at bases of excavated trees. Favorite food is carpenter ants. Young are fed regurgitated insects.

male

female pg. 165

COMMON GOLDENEYE
Bucephala clangula

YEAR-ROUND
SUMMER
WINTER

Size: 18½-20" (47-50 cm)

Male: A mostly white duck with a black back and large, puffy green head. Large white spot in front of each bright golden eye. Dark bill.

Female: brown and gray, a large dark brown head, gray body, white collar, bright golden eyes, yellow-tipped dark bill

Juvenile: same as female, but has a dark bill

Nest: cavity; female lines old woodpecker cavity; 1 brood per year

Eggs: 8-10; light green without markings

Incubation: 28-32 days; female incubates

Fledging: 56-59 days; female leads young to food

Migration: complete, to southern coastal states, partial to non-migrator in southern half of Maine

Food: aquatic plants, insects

Compare: Similar to, but larger than, the black and white male Lesser Scaup (pg. 39). Look for the distinctive white mark in front of each golden eye, and a white chest.

Stan's Notes: Known for its loud whistling, produced by its wings in flight. Moves to southern and coastal Maine during winter. In late winter and early spring, male often attracts female through elaborate displays, throwing head backward while uttering a single raspy note. Female will lay eggs in other goldeneye nests, which results in some mothers incubating up to 30 eggs. Received the common name from its obvious bright golden eyes.

BLACK-CROWNED NIGHT-HERON
Nycticorax nycticorax

MIGRATION
SUMMER

Size: 22-27" (56-69 cm)

Male: A stocky, hunched and inactive heron with black back and crown, white belly and gray wings. Long dark bill, short yellow legs and bright red eyes. Breeding adult has two long white plumes on crown.

Female: same as male

Juvenile: golden brown head and back with white spots, streaked breast, yellow orange eyes, brown bill

Nest: platform; female and male build; 1 brood per year

Eggs: 3-5; light blue without markings

Incubation: 24-26 days; female and male incubate

Fledging: 42-48 days; female and male feed young

Migration: complete, to southern coastal states, Mexico and Central America

Food: fish, aquatic insects

Compare: Half the size of Great Blue Heron (pg. 229) when perching. Look for a short-necked heron with a black back and crown.

Stan's Notes: A very secretive bird, this heron is most active near dawn and dusk (crepuscular). It hunts alone, but nests in small colonies. Roosts in trees during the day. Often squawks if disturbed from the daytime roost. Often seen being harassed by other herons during days.

soaring

OSPREY
Pandion haliaetus

SUMMER

Size: 24" (60 cm); up to 5½-foot wingspan

Male: Large eagle-like bird with a white chest and belly, and a nearly black back. White head with a black streak through the eyes. Large wings with black "wrist" marks. Dark bill.

Female: same as male, but larger, with a necklace of brown streaking

Juvenile: similar to adults, with a light tan breast

Nest: platform, often on raised wooden platform; female and male build; 1 brood per year

Eggs: 2-4; white with brown markings

Incubation: 32-42 days; female and male incubate

Fledging: 48-58 days; male and female feed young

Migration: complete, to southern coastal states, Mexico, Central and South America

Food: fish

Compare: Bald Eagle (pg. 55) is on average 10 inches (25 cm) larger, with an all-white head and tail. The juvenile Bald Eagle is brown with white speckles. Look for a white belly and dark stripe through eyes to identify Osprey.

Stan's Notes: Ospreys are in a family all their own. It is the only raptor that plunges into water feet first to catch fish. Can hover for a few seconds before diving. Carries fish in a head-first position for better aerodynamics. Often harassed by Bald Eagles for its catch. In flight, wings are angled (cocked) backward. Nests on man-made towers and in tall dead trees. Recent studies show male and female might mate for life, but don't migrate to same wintering grounds.

winter

breeding

COMMON LOON
Gavia immer

**YEAR-ROUND
SUMMER**

Size: 28-36" (71-90 cm)

Male: Large, familiar black-and-white bird of the lakes. The breeding adult has checkerboard back with white necklace, black head and deep red eyes with long, pointed black bill. Winter has an entirely gray body and bill.

Female: same as male

Juvenile: similar to winter adult, lacks red eyes

Nest: ground, usually at the shoreline; female and male build; 1 brood per year

Eggs: 2; olive brown, occasionally brown markings

Incubation: 26-31 days; female and male incubate

Fledging: 75-80 days; female and male feed young

Migration: complete, to East and Gulf coasts, Mexico

Food: fish, aquatic insects

Compare: Double-crested Cormorant (pg. 21) has a black chest and gray bill with yellow at the base and a hooked tip.

Stan's Notes: A wonderful bird that represents the wildness of the lakes of Maine. Nests across inland Maine, moving to the coast in the winter. Prefers clear lakes because it hunts for fish by eyesight. Legs are set so far back that it has a hard time walking on land, but it is a great swimmer. Its name comes from the Scandinavian term *lom*, meaning "lame," for the awkward way it walks on land. Its wailing call suggests wild laughter, which led to the phrase "crazy as a loon." Young ride on the backs of their swimming parents. Adults perform distraction displays to protect the young. Very sensitive to disturbance during nesting and will abandon the nest.

soaring

juvenile

BALD EAGLE
Haliaeetus leucocephalus

YEAR-ROUND
SUMMER

Size: 31-37" (79-94 cm); up to 7-foot wingspan

Male: Pure white head and tail contrast with dark brown-to-black body and wings. A large, curved yellow bill and yellow feet.

Female: same as male, only slightly larger

Juvenile: dark brown with white spots or speckles throughout body and wings, gray bill

Nest: massive platform, usually in a tree; female and male build; 1 brood per year

Eggs: 2; off-white without markings

Incubation: 34-36 days; female and male incubate

Fledging: 75-90 days; female and male feed young

Migration: complete to partial, to coastal states

Food: fish, carrion, birds (mainly ducks)

Compare: Larger than Turkey Vulture (pg. 19), which lacks adult Bald Eagle's white head and tail. Turkey Vulture has two-toned wings and flies with its wings in a V shape, unlike the straight-out wing position of the Eagle.

Stan's Notes: Driven to near extinction due to DDT poisoning and illegal killing. Now making a comeback in North America. Returns to same nest each year, adding more sticks, enlarging it to massive proportions, at times up to 1,000 pounds (450 kg). In the midair mating ritual, one eagle will flip upside down and lock talons with another. Both tumble, then break apart to continue flight. Thought to mate for life, but will switch mates if not successful reproducing. Juvenile attains the white head and tail at about 4 to 5 years of age.

female pg. 87

male

INDIGO BUNTING
Passerina cyanea

Size:	5½" (14 cm)
Male:	Vibrant blue finch-like bird. Scattered dark markings on wings and tail.
Female:	light brown bird with faint markings
Juvenile:	similar to female
Nest:	cup; female builds; 2 broods per year
Eggs:	3-4; pale blue without markings
Incubation:	12-13 days; female incubates
Fledging:	10-11 days; female feeds young
Migration:	complete, to Mexico, Central America and South America
Food:	insects, seeds, fruit; will visit seed feeders
Compare:	Smaller than male Eastern Bluebird (pg. 63) and lacks Bluebird's rusty red breast.

Stan's Notes: Usually only the males are noticed. Actually a black bird, as it doesn't have any blue pigment in its feathers. As with the Blue Jay, sunlight is refracted within the structure of the bunting's feathers, making them appear blue. Appears iridescent in direct sun. Molts to acquire body feathers with gray tips, which quickly wear off to reveal bright blue plumage in spring. Molts in fall to appear like females during winter. Males often sing from treetops to attract mates. Will come to feeders in spring before insects are plentiful. Mostly seen along woodland edges, feeding on insects. Migrates at night in flocks of five to ten birds. A late migrant, males return before females and juveniles, usually returning to previous year's nest site. Juveniles move to within a mile from birth site.

TREE SWALLOW
Tachycineta bicolor

SUMMER

Size: 5-6" (13-15 cm)

Male: Blue green in the spring and greener in fall. Appears to change color in direct sunlight. A white belly, a notched tail and pointed wing tips.

Female: similar to male, only duller

Juvenile: gray brown with a white belly and grayish breast band

Nest: cavity; female and male line former woodpecker cavity or nest box; 2 broods per year

Eggs: 4-6; white without markings

Incubation: 13-16 days; female incubates

Fledging: 20-24 days; female and male feed young

Migration: complete, to southern coastal states, Mexico and Central America

Food: insects

Compare: Similar color to Purple Martin (pg. 65), but smaller and has white chest and belly. Barn Swallow (pg. 61) has rust belly and deeply forked tail.

Stan's Notes: This swallow is most common along coastal beaches, freshwater ponds and lakes, and agricultural fields. Attracted to your yard with a nesting box. Competes with Eastern Bluebirds for cavities and nest boxes. Will travel great distances to find dropped feathers to line its grass nest. Sometimes seen playing, chasing after dropped feathers. It is often seen flying back and forth across open fields, feeding on insects. Gathers in large flocks to migrate.

BARN SWALLOW
Hirundo rustica

SUMMER

Size: 7" (18 cm)

Male: A sleek swallow with a blue black back, a cinnamon belly and a reddish brown chin. White spots on long forked tail.

Female: same as male, only slightly duller

Juvenile: similar to adults, with a tan belly and chin, and shorter tail

Nest: cup; female and male build; 2 broods a year

Eggs: 4-5; white with brown markings

Incubation: 13-17 days; female incubates

Fledging: 18-23 days; female and male feed young

Migration: complete, to South America

Food: insects, prefers beetles, wasps and flies

Compare: Tree Swallow (pg. 59) has a white belly and chin, and notched tail. The Chimney Swift (pg. 71) has narrow pointed tail with wings longer than the body. The Purple Martin (pg. 65) is nearly 2 inches (5 cm) larger and has a dark purple belly.

Stan's Notes: Of the six swallow species in Maine, this is the only one with a deeply forked tail. Unlike the other swallows, the Barn Swallow rarely glides in flight, so look for continuous flapping. It builds a mud nest using up to 1,000 beak-loads of mud, often in or on barns. Nests in colonies of four to six, but nesting alone is not uncommon. Drinks while flying by skimming water or getting water from wet leaves. It also bathes while flying through the rain or sprinklers.

male

female

EASTERN BLUEBIRD
Sialia sialis

YEAR-ROUND
SUMMER

Size: 7" (18 cm)

Male: Reminiscent of its larger cousin, American Robin, with a rusty red breast and a white belly. Sky blue head, back and tail.

Female: shares rusty red breast and white belly, but is grayer with faint blue tail and wings

Juvenile: similar to female, with spots on chest, blue wing markings

Nest: cavity, old woodpecker cavity or man-made nest box; female builds; 2 broods per year

Eggs: 4-5; pale blue without markings

Incubation: 12-14 days; female incubates

Fledging: 15-18 days; male and female feed young

Migration: complete, to southern states

Food: insects, fruit

Compare: Male Indigo Bunting (pg. 57) is nearly all blue, lacking the rusty red breast. Blue Jay (pg. 67) is considerably larger, with a crest and white markings.

Stan's Notes: A summer resident of open fields and agricultural areas. Once nearly eliminated from Maine due to a lack of nesting cavities, bluebirds have made a remarkable comeback with the aid of bird enthusiasts who have put up thousands of bluebird boxes. Bluebirds like fields, pastures, roadsides and other open habitats. Will perch in trees or on fence posts and wait for grasshoppers. Easily tamed, will come to a shallow dish with mealworms. Gives a distinctive "chur-lee chur chur-lee" song. Young of the first brood help raise young of the second.

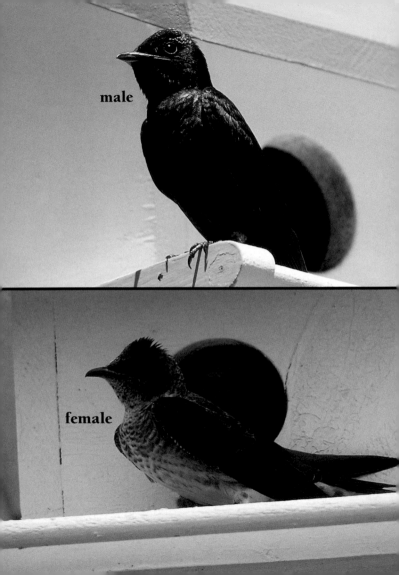

male

female

PURPLE MARTIN
Progne subis

SUMMER

Size: 8½" (22 cm)

Male: A large swallow-shaped bird with a purple head, back and belly. Black wings and tail. Notched tail.

Female: gray purple head and back with a whitish belly, darker wings and tail

Juvenile: same as female

Nest: cavity; female and male line the cavity of house; 1 brood per year

Eggs: 4-5; white without markings

Incubation: 15-18 days; female incubates

Fledging: 26-30 days; male and female feed young

Migration: complete, to South America

Food: insects

Compare: The male is the only swallow with a dark purple belly. Usually only seen in groups.

Stan's Notes: Largest swallow species in North America. Used to nest in tree cavities in Maine, but now it nearly exclusively nests in man-made nesting boxes. Its main diet consists of dragonflies, not mosquitoes as once thought. Often drinks and bathes while flying by skimming water or flying through rain. Returns to the same nest site each year. Males arrive before the females and yearlings. Often nests within 100 feet (30 m) of a human dwelling and, in fact, the most successful colonies are located within this distance. Young strike out to form new colonies. Huge colonies gather in autumn to migrate to South America.

BLUE JAY
Cyanocitta cristata

Size: 12" (30 cm)

Male: Large bright-light-blue and white bird with black necklace. Crest moves up and down at will. White face with a gray belly. White wing bars on blue wings. Black spots and a white tip on blue tail.

Female: same as male

Juvenile: same as adult, only duller

Nest: cup; the female and male build; 1-2 broods per year

Eggs: 4-5; green to blue with brown markings

Incubation: 16-18 days; female incubates

Fledging: 17-21 days; female and male feed young

Migration: non-migrator to partial migrator; will move around to find abundant food source

Food: insects, fruit, carrion, seeds, nuts; comes to seed feeders, and ground feeders with corn

Compare: Eastern Bluebird (pg. 63) is much smaller and lacks the crest. The Belted Kingfisher (pg. 69) lacks the vivid blue coloring and black necklace of Blue Jay.

Stan's Notes: Highly intelligent bird, solving problems, gathering food and communicating more than other birds. Will scream like a hawk to scatter birds at a feeder before approaching. Known as the alarm of the forest, screaming at any intruders in the woods. Is known to eat eggs or young birds from nests of other birds. One of the few birds to cache food. Feathers don't contain blue pigment; refracted sunlight casts blue light.

male

female

BELTED KINGFISHER
Megaceryle alcyon

YEAR-ROUND
SUMMER

Size: 13" (33 cm)

Male: Large blue bird with white belly. Broad blue gray breast band and a ragged crest that is raised and lowered at will. Large head with a long, thick black bill. A small white spot directly in front of red brown eyes. Black wing tips with splashes of white that flash when flying.

Female: same as male, but with rusty breast band in addition to blue gray band, and rusty flanks

Juvenile: similar to female

Nest: cavity; female and male excavate; 1 brood per year

Eggs: 6-7; white without markings

Incubation: 23-24 days; female and male incubate

Fledging: 23-24 days; female and male feed young

Migration: complete, to southern states, Central and South America; winters in coastal Maine

Food: small fish

Compare: Kingfisher is darker blue than the Blue Jay (pg. 67) and has a larger, more ragged crest. Kingfisher is rarely found away from water.

Stan's Notes: Perched on a branch near water, it will dive head-first for small fish and return to the branch to feed. Gives a loud machine-gun-like call. Digs a deep nest cavity in the bank of a river or lake. Parents drop dead fish into water, teaching the young to dive. Can't pass bones through its digestive tract; regurgitates bone pellets after meals. Mates recognize each other by call.

CHIMNEY SWIFT
Chaetura pelagica

SUMMER

Size:	5" (13 cm)
Male:	Nondescript, swallow-shaped bird, usually only seen flying. Long, thin all-brown body with a pointed tail and head. Long swept-back wings are longer than body.
Female:	same as male
Juvenile:	same as adult
Nest:	half cup; female and male build; 1 brood per year
Eggs:	4-5; white without markings
Incubation:	19-21 days; female and male incubate
Fledging:	28-30 days; female and male feed young
Migration:	complete, to South America
Food:	insects caught in air
Compare:	Considerably smaller than Purple Martin (pg. 65) and lacks the iridescent purple of the Martin. Barn Swallow (pg. 61) has a forked tail, compared with the pointed tail of Chimney Swift. Tree Swallow (pg. 59) has a white belly and blue green back.

Stan's Notes: One of the fastest fliers in the bird world. Spends all day flying, rarely perching. Bathes and drinks by skimming across water surfaces. Unique in-flight twittering call is often heard before bird is seen. Flies in groups, feeding on flying insects nearly 100 feet (30 m) in the air. Often called Flying Cigar due to its pointed body shape. Hundreds roost in large chimneys, hence the common name. Builds nest with tiny twigs, cementing it with saliva, attaching it to inside of chimney or hollow tree. Usually only one nest per chimney.

BROWN CREEPER
Certhia americana

YEAR-ROUND

Size: 5" (13 cm)

Male: Small, thin, nearly camouflaged brown bird. White from chin to belly. White eyebrows. Long stiff tail. Dark eyes. Thin curved bill.

Female: same as male

Juvenile: same as adult

Nest: cup; female builds; unknown how many broods per year

Eggs: 5-6; white with tiny brown markings

Incubation: 14-17 days; female incubates, male feeds female during incubation

Fledging: 13-16 days; female and male feed young

Migration: partial migrator to non-migrator

Food: insects, nuts, seeds

Compare: Creeps up tree trunks, not down, like the White-breasted Nuthatch (pg. 191). Watch for the Brown Creeper to fly from the top of one trunk to the bottom of another, then work its way to the top, looking for insects. Slightly larger than Red-breasted Nuthatch (pg. 187), with a similar white stripe above the eyes, but the Brown Creeper has a white belly, long tail and lacks a black crown.

Stan's Notes: This bird utilizes its camouflage coloring to defend itself, spreading out flat on a branch or tree trunk without moving. Young are able to follow their parents, creeping soon after fledging. Commonly found in wooded areas. Often builds nest behind loose bark of dead or dying trees.

CHESTNUT-SIDED WARBLER
Setophaga pensylvanica

SUMMER

Size: 5" (13 cm)

Male: A colorful combination of a yellow cap and black mask set against a white face, chin, breast and belly. Two yellow wing bars on gray wings. Chestnut-colored flanks.

Female: similar to male, flanks are duller brown

Juvenile: similar to female, has a lime green head and back, a white eye-ring, bright yellow wing bars, lacks chestnut sides

Nest: cup; female builds; 1 brood per year

Eggs: 3-5; white with brown markings

Incubation: 12-13 days; female incubates

Fledging: 10-12 days; female and male feed young

Migration: complete, to Central America

Food: insects, berries

Compare: Shares yellow cap with the Yellow-rumped Warbler (pg. 193), but lacks yellow sides and rump. The Yellow Warbler (pg. 275) is nearly all yellow and lacks Chestnut-sided's white chest and chestnut flanks.

Stan's Notes: Prefers an open, young aspen forest. Often attracted to backyard water gardens during spring and fall migrations. Look for this attractive warbler in spring, hopping high in the branches while it hunts for insects. You will usually only get a glimpse of this fast-moving warbler. Will hold tail in an uplifted position, showing its white undertail. Not uncommon for it to approach humans in defense of a nest site.

male

female

COMMON REDPOLL
Acanthis flammea

WINTER

Size: 5" (13 cm)

Male: A small sparrow-like bird with a bright red crown and black spot on the chin. Heavily streaked back and a splash of raspberry red on chest.

Female: same as male, but lacking raspberry red on the chest

Juvenile: browner than adults, lacks a red crown, has dark streaks on chest

Nest: cup; female builds; 1 brood (sometimes 2) per year

Eggs: 4-5; pale green with purple markings

Incubation: 10-11 days; female incubates

Fledging: 11-12 days; female and male feed young

Migration: irruptive; moves into Maine from Canada in some winters

Food: seeds, insects; will come to seed feeders

Compare: Slightly smaller than the male Purple Finch (pg. 247), lacking male Purple Finch's red back and rump. Similar to the male House Finch (pg. 245), but lacks the orange red rump. Look for the bright red crown and black spot under the bill.

Stan's Notes: After summering in the far reaches of Canada, it winters in Maine. Winter flocks of up to 100 individuals are not uncommon. Bathes in snow or open water in winter. Much like the Black-capped Chickadee, it can be tamed and hand fed.

CHIPPING SPARROW
Spizella passerina

SUMMER

Size: 5" (13 cm)

Male: Small gray brown sparrow with a clear gray chest, rusty crown, white eyebrows with a black eye line, thin gray black bill and two faint wing bars.

Female: same as male

Juvenile: similar to adult, has a streaked breast, lacks the rusty crown

Nest: cup; female builds; 2 broods per year

Eggs: 3-5; blue green with brown markings

Incubation: 11-14 days; female incubates

Fledging: 10-12 days; female and male feed young

Migration: complete, to southern states, Mexico and Central America

Food: insects, seeds; will come to ground feeders

Compare: Smaller than Song Sparrow (pg. 91), which has a heavily streaked chest. Female House Finch (pg. 83) also has a streaked breast, compared with the unmarked breast of the Chipping Sparrow.

Stan's Notes: This summer resident in Maine is a common garden or yard bird, often seen feeding on dropped seeds beneath feeders. Gathers in large family groups in autumn to feed in preparation for migration. Migrates at night in flocks of 20 to 30 birds. Received its common name from the male's fast "chip" call. Often just called Chippy. Nest is placed low in dense shrubs and almost always is lined with animal hair.

PINE SISKIN
Spinus pinus

Size: 5" (13 cm)

Male: Small brown finch. Heavily streaked back, breast and belly. Yellow wing bars. Yellow at base of tail. Thin bill.

Female: similar to male, with less yellow

Juvenile: similar to adult, light yellow tinge over the breast and chin

Nest: modified cup; female constructs; 2 broods per year

Eggs: 3-4; greenish blue with brown markings

Incubation: 12-13 days; female incubates

Fledging: 14-15 days; female and male feed young

Migration: non-migrator to irruptive; moves around the United States in search of food

Food: seeds, insects; will come to seed feeders

Compare: Female American Goldfinch (pg. 269) lacks streaks and has white wing bars. Female House Finch (pg. 83) has a streaked chest, but lacks yellow wing bars. Female Purple Finch (pg. 95) has bold white eyebrows.

Stan's Notes: Usually considered a winter finch, it is a year-round breeding resident in Maine. It can be more conspicuous in some years, and absent in some areas in other years. Seen in flocks of up to 20 individuals, often with other finch species. Travels and breeds in small groups. Comes to thistle feeders. Male feeds female during incubation. Juveniles lose yellow tint by late summer of first year. Builds nest toward ends of coniferous branches, where needles are dense, helping to conceal. Nests are often only a few feet apart.

female

male pg. 245

HOUSE FINCH
Haemorhous mexicanus

Size:	5" (13 cm)
Female:	A plain brown bird with a heavily streaked white chest.
Male:	orange red face, chest and rump, a brown cap, brown marking behind eyes, brown wings streaked with white, streaked belly
Juvenile:	similar to female
Nest:	cup, sometimes in cavities; female builds; 2 broods per year
Eggs:	4-5; pale blue, lightly marked
Incubation:	12-14 days; female incubates
Fledging:	15-19 days; female and male feed young
Migration:	non-migrator to partial migrator; will move around to find food
Food:	seeds, fruit, leaf buds; will visit seed feeders
Compare:	The female Purple Finch (pg. 95) is very similar, but has bold white eyebrows. The female American Goldfinch (pg. 269) has a clear chest and white wing bars. Similar to Pine Siskin (pg. 81), but lacks yellow wing bars and has a much larger bill than Siskin.

Stan's Notes: Very social bird. Visits feeders in small flocks. Likes nesting in hanging flower baskets. Incubating female is fed by the male. Has a loud, cheerful warbling song. House Finches that were originally introduced to Long Island, New York, from the western U.S. in the 1940s have since populated the entire eastern U.S. Now found throughout the country. Suffers from a fatal eye disease that causes eyes to crust over.

HOUSE WREN
Troglodytes aedon

SUMMER

Size: 5" (13 cm)

Male: A small all-brown bird with lighter brown markings on tail and wings. Slightly curved brown bill. Often holds its tail erect.

Female: same as male

Juvenile: same as adult

Nest: cavity; female and male line just about any cavity; 2 broods per year

Eggs: 4-6; tan with brown markings

Incubation: 10-13 days; female and male incubate

Fledging: 12-15 days; female and male feed young

Migration: complete, to southern states and Mexico

Food: insects

Compare: Wren's long curved bill and long upturned tail differentiates it from sparrows. Lack of eyebrows distinguishes it from other wrens.

Stan's Notes: A prolific songster, it will sing from dawn until dusk during the mating season. Easily attracted to nest boxes. In spring, the male chooses several prospective nesting cavities and places a few small twigs in each. Female inspects each, chooses one, and finishes the nest building. She will completely fill the nest cavity with uniformly small twigs, then line a small depression at back of cavity with pine needles and grass. Often has trouble fitting long twigs through nest cavity hole. Tries many different directions and approaches until successful.

female

male pg. 57

INDIGO BUNTING
Passerina cyanea

SUMMER

Size: 5½" (14 cm)

Female: Light brown finch-like bird. Faint streaking on a light tan chest. Wings have a very faint blue cast with indistinct wing bars.

Male: vibrant blue finch-like bird, scattered dark markings on wings and tail

Juvenile: similar to female

Nest: cup; female builds; 2 broods per year

Eggs: 3-4; pale blue without markings

Incubation: 12-13 days; female incubates

Fledging: 10-11 days; female feeds young

Migration: complete, to Mexico, Central America and South America

Food: insects, seeds, fruit; will visit seed feeders

Compare: Similar to female finches. Female American Goldfinch (pg. 269) has white wing bars. The female Purple Finch (pg. 95) has white eyebrows and a heavily streaked chest. The female House Finch (pg. 83) also has a heavily streaked chest.

Stan's Notes: A secretive bird, usually only the male buntings are seen. Males often sing from treetops to attract mates. Will come to feeders in the spring before insects are plentiful. Mostly seen along woodland edges, feeding on insects. Migrates at night in flocks of five to ten birds. A late migrant, males return before females and juveniles. Juveniles move to within a mile from birth site.

male pg. 195

female

DARK-EYED JUNCO
Junco hyemalis

YEAR-ROUND

Size: 5½" (14 cm)

Female: A round, dark-eyed bird with tan-to-brown chest, head and back. White belly. Ivory-to-pink bill. Since the outermost tail feathers are white, tail appears as a white V in flight.

Male: same as female, only slate gray to charcoal

Juvenile: similar to female, but has a streaked breast and head

Nest: cup; female and male construct; 2 broods per year

Eggs: 3-5; white with reddish brown markings

Incubation: 12-13 days; female incubates

Fledging: 10-13 days; male and female feed young

Migration: complete, across the United States, non-migrator in Maine

Food: seeds, insects; will come to seed feeders

Compare: Rarely confused with any other bird. Small flocks feed under bird feeders in winter.

Stan's Notes: A year-round resident in Maine, but usually is more commonly seen during the winter. Usually seen on the ground in small flocks. Migrates from Canada to Maine and beyond, swelling resident populations. Females tend to migrate farther south than males. It adheres to a rigid social hierarchy, with dominant birds chasing the less dominant birds. Look for white outer tail feathers flashing while in flight. Most comfortable on the ground, juncos will use both feet to "double-scratch," exposing seeds and insects. Consumes many weed seeds. Several junco species have now been combined into one, simply called Dark-eyed Junco.

SONG SPARROW
Melospiza melodia

Size: 5-6" (13-15 cm)

Male: Common brown sparrow with heavy dark streaks on breast coalescing into a central dark spot.

Female: same as male

Juvenile: similar to adult, finely streaked breast, lacks a central spot

Nest: cup; female builds; 2 broods per year

Eggs: 3-4; pale blue to green with reddish brown markings

Incubation: 12-14 days; female incubates

Fledging: 9-12 days; female and male feed young

Migration: complete, to southern states, non-migrator in southern Maine

Food: insects, seeds; rarely visits seed feeders

Compare: Similar to other brown sparrows. Look for a heavily streaked chest with central dark spot.

Stan's Notes: Many Song Sparrow subspecies or varieties, but dark central spot carries through each variant. While the female builds another nest for a second brood, the male sparrow often takes over feeding the young. Returns to a similar area each year, defending a small territory by singing from thick shrubs. A common host of the Brown-headed Cowbird. Ground feeders, look for them to scratch simultaneously with both feet to expose seeds. Unlike many other sparrow species, Song Sparrows rarely flock together.

YEAR-ROUND
SUMMER

HOUSE SPARROW
Passer domesticus

YEAR-ROUND

Size: 6" (15 cm)

Male: Medium sparrow-like bird with large black spot on throat extending down to the chest. Brown back and single white wing bars. A gray belly and crown.

Female: all-light-brown bird, slightly smaller, lacks the black throat patch and single wing bars

Juvenile: similar to female

Nest: domed cup nest, within cavity; female and male build; 2-3 broods per year

Eggs: 4-6; white with brown markings

Incubation: 10-12 days; female incubates

Fledging: 14-17 days; female and male feed young

Migration: non-migrator; moves around to find food

Food: seeds, insects, fruit; comes to seed feeders

Compare: Lacks the rusty crown of Chipping Sparrow (pg. 79). Look for male House Sparrow's black bib. Female has a clear chest and no marking on head (cap).

Stan's Notes: One of the first bird songs heard in cities in spring. A familiar city bird, nearly always in small flocks. Also found on farms. Introduced from Europe to Central Park, New York, in 1850, it is now found throughout North America. Related to Old World sparrows; not related to any sparrows in the United States. Constructs an oversized domed nest with scraps of plastic, paper, dried grass and whatever else is available. An aggressive bird that will kill the young of other birds in order to take over a cavity.

male pg. 247

female

YEAR-ROUND

PURPLE FINCH
Haemorhous purpureus

Size: 6" (15 cm)

Female: A brown bird with a heavily streaked white chest. Prominent white eyebrows.

Male: raspberry red head, cap, breast, back and rump, brownish wings and tail

Juvenile: same as female

Nest: cup; female and male build; 1 brood a year

Eggs: 4-5; greenish blue with brown markings

Incubation: 12-13 days; female incubates

Fledging: 13-14 days; female and male feed young

Migration: non-migrator to irruptive; moves around in search of food

Food: seeds, insects, fruit; comes to seed feeders

Compare: Female House Finch (pg. 83) lacks female Purple Finch's white eyebrows. Pine Siskin (pg. 81) has yellow wing bars and a much smaller bill than Purple Finch. The female American Goldfinch (pg. 269) has a clear chest and white wing bars.

Stan's Notes: A year-round resident throughout Maine. Common in non-residential areas (prefers open woods or woodland edges), it has been replaced in cities by House Finches. Feeds primarily on seeds, with ash tree seeds a very important food source. Will visit seed feeders along with House Finches, making it hard to tell them apart. A rich loud song, with a distinctive "tic" note made only in flight. Travels in flocks of up to 50. Not a purple color, the Latin species name *purpureus* means "purple" or other reddish colors.

WHITE-THROATED SPARROW
Zonotrichia albicollis

YEAR-ROUND
SUMMER

Size: 6-7" (15-18 cm)

Male: A brown bird with gray tan chest and belly. Small yellow spot between the eyes (lore). Distinctive white or tan throat patch. White or tan stripes alternate with black stripes on crown. Color of the throat patch and crown stripes match.

Female: same as male

Juvenile: similar to adult, gray throat and eyebrows with heavily streaked chest

Nest: cup; female builds; 1 brood per year

Eggs: 4-6; color varies from greenish to bluish to creamy white with red brown markings

Incubation: 11-14 days; female incubates

Fledging: 10-12 days; female and male feed young

Migration: complete, to southern states and Mexico

Food: insects, seeds, fruit; visits ground feeders

Compare: The White-crowned Sparrow (pg. 99) lacks the throat patch and yellow lore. The Song Sparrow (pg. 91) has a central spot on the chest and lacks the striped pattern on head.

Stan's Notes: There are two color variations (polymorphic) of the White-throated Sparrow: white-striped or tan-striped. Studies have indicated the white-striped adults tend to mate with the tan-striped birds. No indication why. A summer resident, but more abundant during migration, when birds from farther north move through the state. Can be seen at ground feeders. Nests are built on the ground underneath small trees in bogs and coniferous forests.

juvenile

MIGRATION

WHITE-CROWNED SPARROW
Zonotrichia leucophrys

Size:	6½-7½" (16-19 cm)
Male:	A brown sparrow with a gray breast and a black-and-white striped crown. Small, thin pink bill.
Female:	same as male
Juvenile:	similar to adult, with brown stripes on the head instead of white
Nest:	cup; female builds; 2 broods per year
Eggs:	3-5; color varies from greenish to bluish to whitish with red brown markings
Incubation:	11-14 days; female incubates
Fledging:	8-12 days; male and female feed young
Migration:	complete, to southern states and Mexico
Food:	insects, seeds, berries; visits ground feeders
Compare:	The White-throated Sparrow (pg. 97) has a white or tan throat patch, and yellow spot between eyes and bill, with a blackish bill.

Stan's Notes: Usually seen in groups of up to 20 during migration, when it can be seen feeding under seed feeders. Males arrive before the females and establish territories by singing from perches. Feeds on the ground, scratching backward with both feet simultaneously. Male takes most of the responsibility of raising young while female starts the second brood. Only 9 to 12 days separate broods. Doesn't nest in Maine.

SUMMER

SWAINSON'S THRUSH
Catharus ustulatus

Size: 7" (18 cm)

Male: Dusty brown head, back and wings. Brown smudges and spots, especially on its throat, chest and off-white belly. A small, thin two-toned bill, yellow under and black above.

Female: same as male

Juvenile: overall lighter than adult, with less distinct spots on chest

Nest: cup; female builds; 1 brood per year

Eggs: 3-5; pale blue with brown markings

Incubation: 12-14 days; female incubates

Fledging: 10-14 days; female and male feed young

Migration: complete, to Mexico, Central America and South America

Food: insects, fruit

Compare: Similar shape as American Robin (pg. 211), but is smaller and lacks the red breast.

Stan's Notes: A summer resident that is more conspicuous during spring and fall migrations. Often is hard to see because most of the time it stays on the ground in thick vegetation. Song sounds like someone playing a flute. Feeds mostly on insects during spring and summer, adding fruit to its diet in late summer. Nests in shrubs or low in coniferous trees, building a bulky nest that consists of grass, bark and moss, all glued together with mud.

female

male pg. 27

ROSE-BREASTED GROSBEAK
Pheucticus ludovicianus

SUMMER

Size: 7-8" (18-20 cm)

Female: Plump, heavily streaked brown and white bird with obvious white eyebrows. Orange yellow wing linings.

Male: black-and-white bird with large, triangular rose patch in center of chest, wing linings rosy red, large ivory bill

Juvenile: same as female

Nest: cup; the female and male build; 1-2 broods per year

Eggs: 3-5; blue green with brown markings

Incubation: 13-14 days; female and male incubate

Fledging: 9-12 days; female and male feed young

Migration: complete, to Mexico, Central America and South America

Food: insects, seeds, fruit; comes to seed feeders

Compare: Female looks like a large sparrow. Female is larger and has a more distinctive eyebrow mark than female Purple Finch (pg. 95). The female House Finch (pg. 83) has no eyebrow mark.

Stan's Notes: Seen across Maine, but is more conspicuous during migrations. Often prefers mature deciduous forest for nesting. Both sexes sing, but the male sings much louder and clearer. "Grosbeak" refers to its large bill, used to crush seeds. Late to arrive in spring, early to leave in fall. Males arrive in small groups first, joined by females several days later. When females arrive, males reduce their visits to feeders. Young birds visit feeders with adults after fledging.

male
pg. 3

female

SUMMER

EASTERN TOWHEE
Pipilo erythrophthalmus

Size: 7-8" (18-20 cm)

Female: A mostly light brown bird. Rusty red brown sides and white belly. Long brown tail with white tip. Short, stout, pointed bill and rich red eyes. White wing patches flash in flight.

Male: similar to female, but is black, not brown

Juvenile: light brown, a heavily streaked head, chest and belly, long dark tail with white tip

Nest: cup; female builds; 2 broods per year

Eggs: 3-4; creamy white with brown markings

Incubation: 12-13 days; female incubates

Fledging: 10-12 days; male and female feed young

Migration: complete, southern states, South America

Food: insects, seeds, fruit; visits ground feeders

Compare: Slightly smaller than the American Robin (pg. 211). Female Rose-breasted Grosbeak (pg. 103) has a heavily streaked breast and white eyebrows.

Stan's Notes: Common name comes from its distinctive "tow-hee" call given by both sexes. Mostly known for its characteristic call that sounds like, "Drink-your-tea!" Seen hopping backward with both feet (bilateral scratching), raking up leaf litter in search of insects and seeds. The female broods, but the male does the most feeding of young. White-eyed form in southern states, red-eyed elsewhere.

HORNED LARK
Eremophila alpestris

YEAR-ROUND

Size: 7-8" (18-20 cm)

Male: A sleek tan-to-brown bird. Black necklace with a yellow chin and black bill. Two tiny "horns" on top of the head can be difficult to see. Black tail with white outer feathers noticeable in flight.

Female: same as male, only duller, "horns" are even less noticeable

Juvenile: lacks the black markings and yellow chin, doesn't form "horns" until second year

Nest: ground; female builds; 2-3 broods per year

Eggs: 3-4; gray with brown markings

Incubation: 11-12 days; female incubates

Fledging: 9-12 days; female and male feed young

Migration: non-migrator to partial migrator in Maine

Food: seeds, insects

Compare: Smaller than Meadowlark (pg. 289), which shares the black necklace and yellow chin. Look for the black marks in front of eyes.

Stan's Notes: The only true lark native to North America. A year-round resident, moving around in winter to find food. Larks are birds of open ground. Common in rural areas, often seen in large flocks. Population increased in North America over the past 100 years due to clearing land for farming. May have up to three broods per year because they get such an early start. Females will perform a fluttering distraction display if the nest is disturbed. Females can renest about seven days after the brood fledges. The name "Lark" comes from the Middle English word *laverock*, or "a lark."

1 year old

Bohemian
Waxwing

CEDAR WAXWING
Bombycilla cedrorum

YEAR-ROUND
SUMMER

Size: 7½" (19 cm)

Male: Very sleek-looking gray-to-brown bird with pointed crest, light yellow belly and bandit-like black mask. Tip of tail is bright yellow and the tips of wings look as if they have been dipped in red wax.

Female: same as male

Juvenile: grayish with a heavily streaked chest, lacks red wing tips, black mask and sleek look

Nest: cup; female and male build; 1 brood a year, occasionally 2

Eggs: 4-6; pale blue with brown markings

Incubation: 10-12 days; female incubates

Fledging: 14-18 days; female and male feed young

Migration: partial migrator; moves around to find food

Food: cedar cones, fruit, insects

Compare: Female Cardinal (pg. 119) has large red bill. Its larger, less common cousin, Bohemian Waxwing (see inset), has white on wings and rust under tail.

Stan's Notes: The name is derived from its red wax-like wing tips and preference for eating small blueberry-like cones of the cedar. Mostly seen in flocks, moving from area to area, looking for berries. Wanders in winter to find available food supplies. Seen more often in winter because naked branches reveal its presence. In summer, before berries are abundant, it feeds on insects. Spends most of its time at the tops of tall trees. Listen for the very high-pitched "sreee" whistling sounds it constantly makes. Obtains mask after first year.

male pg. 5

female

BROWN-HEADED COWBIRD
Molothrus ater

Size: 7½" (19 cm)

Female: Dull brown bird with no obvious markings. Pointed, sharp gray bill.

Male: glossy black bird, chocolate brown head

Juvenile: similar to female, only dull gray color and a streaked chest

Nest: no nest; lays eggs in nests of other birds

Eggs: 5-7; white with brown markings

Incubation: 10-13 days; host bird incubates eggs

Fledging: 10-11 days; host birds feed young

Migration: complete, to southern states

Food: insects, seeds; will come to seed feeders

Compare: Female Red-winged Blackbird (pg. 121) is slightly larger and has white eyebrows and a streaked chest. European Starling (pg. 7) has speckles and a shorter tail.

Stan's Notes: A member of the blackbird family. Of more than 100 species of parasitic birds worldwide, this is the only parasitic bird in Maine, laying all eggs in host birds' nests, leaving others to raise its young. Cowbirds are known to have laid eggs in nests of over 200 species of birds. Some birds reject cowbird eggs, but most incubate them and raise the young, even to the exclusion of their own. Look for warblers and other birds feeding young birds twice their own size. At one time cowbirds followed bison to feed on the insects attracted to the animals.

SUMMER

WOOD THRUSH
Hylocichla mustelina

Size: 8" (20 cm)

Male: Reddish brown head, back and wings with color fading into a brown tail. A distinctive white breast, belly and sides, covered with black spots. White ring around black eyes, obvious on a black-streaked white face.

Female: same as male

Juvenile: similar to adult

Nest: cup; female builds; 1-2 broods per year

Eggs: 2-4; greenish blue without markings

Incubation: 13-14 days; female incubates

Fledging: 11-12 days; female and male feed young

Migration: complete, to Central and South America

Food: insects, fruit

Compare: Similar body shape as the American Robin (pg. 211), but lacks the Robin's red breast. Similar rusty color as the Brown Thrasher (pg. 129), but Brown Thrasher has a much longer rusty red tail and bright yellow eyes, compared with the shorter brown tail and black eyes of Wood Thrush.

Stan's Notes: One of the easier thrushes to identify due to the large dark spots on breast and belly. Well known for its liquid flute-like calls, heard deep within woodlots throughout Maine. Returns to the same woodland every year during April to May. Often seen on the ground, hopping around like a robin in search of insects.

winter

breeding

SPOTTED SANDPIPER
Actitis macularius

MIGRATION

Size: 8" (20 cm)

Male: Olive brown back. Long bill and long dull yellow legs. White chest. A white line over the eyes. Breeding adult has black spots on chest. Winter adult lacks breast spots.

Female: same as male

Juvenile: similar to winter adult, with a darker bill

Nest: ground; male builds; 2 broods per year

Eggs: 3-4; brownish with brown markings

Incubation: 20-24 days; male incubates

Fledging: 17-21 days; male feeds young

Migration: complete, to southern coastal states, Mexico, Central and South America

Food: aquatic insects

Compare: Much smaller than the Greater Yellowlegs (pg. 141). Look for Spotted Sandpiper to bob its tail up and down while standing. Look for breeding Sandpiper's black spots extending from chest to abdomen.

Stan's Notes: One of the few shorebirds that will dive underwater if pursued. Able to fly straight up out of the water. Flies with wings held in a cup-like arc, rarely lifting them above a horizontal plane. Constantly bobs its tail while standing and walks as if delicately balanced. Female mates with multiple males and lays eggs in up to five different nests. Male incubates and cares for young. In winter plumage, it lacks spots.

NORTHERN SAW-WHET OWL
Aegolius acadicus

YEAR-ROUND

Size: 8" (20 cm); up to 17-inch wingspan

Male: Small tawny brown owl with wide vertical rusty brown streaks on a white breast and belly. Distinctive light marks on back and wings. Short tail. A white face, yellow eyes and small dark bill.

Female: same as male

Juvenile: dark brown with a light brown belly

Nest: cavity, former woodpecker cavity; does not add any nesting material; 1 brood

Eggs: 5-6; white without markings

Incubation: 26-28 days; female and male incubate

Fledging: 27-34 days; male and female feed young

Migration: partial migrator to non-migrator

Food: mice, small birds, insects

Compare: Smaller than Barred Owl (pg. 169), which has dark eyes. Great Horned Owl (pg. 171) is much larger, with large and obvious ear tufts, which the Saw-whet Owl lacks.

Stan's Notes: A resident throughout Maine, moving about in fall to the southern portion of the state. Our smallest owl, it is not often recognized as an owl because of its diminutive size. Usually found in mixed coniferous-deciduous forest. Strictly a nighttime hunter. Often roosts in cavities in conifers, thick vegetation or Wood Duck nesting boxes. Has relatively long wings for such a small raptor. The common name comes from its rarely heard call, a repeated low raspy whistle that is reminiscent of a saw blade being sharpened. Can be very tame and approachable.

117

male pg. 251

female

juvenile

NORTHERN CARDINAL
Cardinalis cardinalis

YEAR-ROUND

Size: 8-9" (20-22.5 cm)

Female: Buff brown bird with tinges of red on crest and wings, a black mask and large red bill

Male: red bird with a black mask extending from face down to chin and throat, large red bill and crest

Juvenile: same as female, but with a blackish gray bill

Nest: cup; female builds; 2-3 broods per year

Eggs: 3-4; bluish white with brown markings

Incubation: 12-13 days; female and male incubate

Fledging: 9-10 days; female and male feed young

Migration: non-migrator

Food: seeds, insects, fruit; comes to seed feeders

Compare: Cedar Waxwing (pg. 109) has a small dark bill. Female Cardinal appears similar to the juvenile Cardinal. Look for female's bright red bill.

Stan's Notes: A familiar backyard bird. Look for the male feeding female during courtship. Male feeds young of the first brood by himself while female builds second nest. The name comes from the Latin word *cardinalis*, which denotes importance. Very territorial in spring, it will fight its own reflection in a window. Non-territorial during winter, gathering in small flocks of up to 20 birds. Both the female and male sing, and can be heard anytime of year. Listen for its "whata-cheer-cheer-cheer" territorial call in spring.

male pg. 9

female

RED-WINGED BLACKBIRD
Agelaius phoeniceus

SUMMER

Size: 8½" (22 cm)

Female: Heavily streaked brown bird with a pointed brown bill and white eyebrows.

Male: jet black bird with red and yellow patches on upper wings, pointed black bill

Juvenile: same as female

Nest: cup; female builds; 2-3 broods per year

Eggs: 3-4; bluish green with brown markings

Incubation: 10-12 days; female incubates

Fledging: 11-14 days; female and male feed young

Migration: complete, to southern states

Food: seeds, insects; will come to seed feeders

Compare: The slightly larger female Rusty Blackbird (pg. 207) and the slightly smaller female Brown-headed Cowbird (pg. 111) lack the prominent white eyebrows and streaks on breast. Similar to the female Rose-breasted Grosbeak (pg. 103), but Red-winged has a thinner body and pointed bill.

Stan's Notes: One of the most widespread and numerous birds in Maine. It's a sure sign of spring when Red-winged Blackbirds return to the marshes. Flocks of up to 10,000 birds have been reported. Males return before females and defend territories by singing from tops of surrounding vegetation. The males repeat call from tops of cattails while showing off their red and yellow shoulder patches. Females choose mate and usually nest over shallow water in thick stands of cattails. Red-wingeds feed mostly on seeds during fall and spring, switching to insects in summer.

in flight

COMMON NIGHTHAWK
Chordeiles minor

SUMMER

Size: 9" (22.5 cm)

Male: A camouflaged brown and white bird with white chin. A distinctive white band across wings and the tail, seen only in flight.

Female: similar to male, but with tan chin, lacks the white tail band

Juvenile: similar to female

Nest: no nest; lays eggs on the ground, usually on rocks, or on rooftop; 1 brood per year

Eggs: 2; cream with lavender markings

Incubation: 19-20 days; female and male incubate

Fledging: 20-21 days; female and male feed young

Migration: complete, to South America

Food: insects caught in air

Compare: Male Whip-poor-will (pg. 125) is similar in size, but much browner. Look for the white chin and wing band of Nighthawk in flight. Chimney Swift (pg. 71) is much smaller. Look for Nighthawk's characteristic flap-flap-flap-glide flight pattern.

Stan's Notes: Usually only seen flying at dusk or after sunset, but not uncommon for it to be sitting on a fence post, sleeping during the day. A very noisy bird, repeating a "peenting" call during flight. Alternates slow wing beats with bursts of quick wing beats. Prolific insect eater. Prefers gravel rooftops for nesting in cities and nests on the ground in country. Male's distinctive springtime mating ritual is a steep diving flight terminated with a loud popping noise. One of the first birds to migrate each fall, starting in August.

SUMMER

WHIP-POOR-WILL
Antrostomas vociferus

Size: 10" (25 cm)

Male: Mottled brown and black. Distinctive black chin and a white U-shaped throat marking.

Female: same as male, but has a brown chin and tan throat marking

Juvenile: similar to adult of the same sex

Nest: no nest; lays eggs on ground; 1-2 broods per year

Eggs: 2; white with brown markings

Incubation: 19-20 days; female and male incubate

Fledging: 18-20 days; female and male feed young

Migration: complete, to Mexico, Central America and South America

Food: insects

Compare: Male Common Nighthawk (pg. 123) has a distinctive white band across wings (seen in flight), which the Whip-poor-will lacks. Nighthawk is commonly seen flying, while Whip-poor-will is rarely seen flying.

Stan's Notes: A common bird in Maine, although it is rarely seen. Its repetitive nocturnal "whip-poor-will" call, usually heard only in the spring, is loved by many and hated by others. Nothing can be done to stop the nocturnal calling despite how much sleep you are losing. Generally found in woodland, Whip-poor-wills sit parallel on a branch during the day. They don't build nests, but lay eggs on the ground, selecting sites along forest edges. The male will care for its young if the female starts a second brood.

KILLDEER
Charadrius vociferus

Size: 11" (28 cm)

Male: An upland shorebird with two black bands around the neck like a necklace. A brown back and white belly. Bright reddish orange rump, visible in flight.

Female: same as male

Juvenile: similar to adult, with only one neck band

Nest: ground; male builds; 2 broods per year

Eggs: 3-5; tan with brown markings

Incubation: 24-28 days; male and female incubate

Fledging: 25 days; male and female lead their young to food

Migration: complete, to southern states, Mexico and Central America

Food: insects

Compare: The Spotted Sandpiper (pg. 115) is found around water and lacks the two neck bands of the Killdeer.

Stan's Notes: The only shorebird with two black neck bands. It is known for its broken wing impression, which draws intruders away from nest. Once clear of the nest, the Killdeer takes flight. Nests are only a slight depression in a gravel area, often very difficult to see. Young look like miniature adults on stilts when first hatched. Able to follow parents and peck for insects soon after birth. Is technically classified as a shorebird, but doesn't live at the shore. Often found in vacant fields or along railroads. Has a very distinctive "kill-deer" call.

BROWN THRASHER
Toxostoma rufum

SUMMER

Size: 11" (28 cm)

Male: A rusty red bird with long tail and heavily streaked breast and belly. Two white wing bars. Long curved bill. Bright yellow eyes.

Female: same as male

Juvenile: same as adult, but eye color is grayish

Nest: cup; female and male build; 2 broods a year

Eggs: 4-5; pale blue with brown markings

Incubation: 11-14 days; female and male incubate

Fledging: 10-13 days; female and male feed young

Migration: complete, to southern states

Food: insects, fruit

Compare: Slightly larger in size and similar in shape to the American Robin (pg. 211) and Gray Catbird (pg. 205), but the Thrasher has a streaked breast and rusty color. The Wood Thrush (pg. 113) has a shorter brown tail and black eyes, compared with Thrasher's longer rusty red tail and yellow eyes.

Stan's Notes: Summer resident in the southern half of the state. A prodigious songster, it is often found in thick shrubs where it sings deliberate musical phrases, repeating each twice. The male has the largest documented song repertoire of all North American birds, with over 1,100 song types. Often seen quickly flying or running in and out of dense shrubs. Noisy feeding due to habit of turning over leaves, small rocks and branches. This bird is more abundant in the central Great Plains than anywhere else in North America.

male

female

AMERICAN KESTREL
Falco sparverius

YEAR-ROUND
SUMMER

Size: 10-12" (25-30 cm); up to 2-foot wingspan

Male: Rusty brown back and tail. A white breast with dark spots. Double black vertical lines on white face. Blue gray wings. Distinctive wide black band with a white edge on tip of rusty tail.

Female: similar to male, but slightly larger, has rusty brown wings and dark bands on tail

Juvenile: same as adult of the same sex

Nest: cavity; doesn't build a nest within; 1 brood per year

Eggs: 4-5; white with brown markings

Incubation: 29-31 days; male and female incubate

Fledging: 30-31 days; female and male feed young

Migration: partial migrator

Food: insects, small mammals and birds, reptiles

Compare: Similar to other falcons. Look for the two vertical black stripes on face of Kestrel. No other small bird of prey has rusty-colored back or tail.

Stan's Notes: Most migrate, but some remain in urban settings in Maine, feeding on mice along roads. Was known as Sparrow Hawk due to its small size. Could be called Grasshopper Hawk because it eats many grasshoppers. Hovers near roads before diving for prey. Adapts quickly to a wooden nesting box. Has pointed swept-back wings, seen in flight. Perches nearly upright. Unusual raptor in that males and females have quite different markings. Watch for them to pump their tails up and down after landing on perches.

female

male

NORTHERN FLICKER
Colaptes auratus

YEAR-ROUND
SUMMER

Size: 12" (30 cm)

Male: Brown and black woodpecker with a large white rump patch visible only when flying. Black necklace above a speckled breast. Red spot on nape of neck and black mustache.

Female: same as male, but lacking a black mustache

Juvenile: same as adult of the same sex

Nest: cavity; female and male excavate; 1 brood per year

Eggs: 5-8; white without markings

Incubation: 11-14 days; female and male incubate

Fledging: 25-28 days; female and male feed young

Migration: complete, to southern states

Food: insects, especially ants and beetles

Compare: Yellow-bellied Sapsucker (pg. 29) is smaller, with red chin and forehead. Flickers are the only brown-backed woodpeckers in Maine.

Stan's Notes: This is the only woodpecker to regularly feed on the ground. Preferring ants and beetles, it produces an antacid saliva to neutralize the acidic defense of ants. Male usually selects nest site, taking up to 12 days to excavate. Some have had success attracting flickers to nest boxes stuffed with sawdust. In flight, flashes golden yellow under the wings and tail, undulates deeply and gives a loud "wacka-wacka" call.

MOURNING DOVE
Zenaida macroura

YEAR-ROUND
MIGRATION
SUMMER

Size: 12" (30 cm)

Male: Smooth fawn-colored dove with gray patch on the head. Iridescent pink, green around neck. A single black spot behind and below eyes. Black spots on wings and tail. Pointed wedge-shaped tail with white edges.

Female: similar to male, lacking iridescent pink and green neck feathers

Juvenile: spotted and streaked

Nest: platform; female and male build; 2 broods per year

Eggs: 2; white without markings

Incubation: 13-14 days; male and female incubate, the male during day, female at night

Fledging: 12-14 days; female and male feed young

Migration: non-migrator to partial migrator; will move around to find food

Food: seeds; will visit seed and ground feeders

Compare: Smaller than Rock Pigeon (pg. 219), lacking its wide range of color combinations.

Stan's Notes: Name comes from its mournful cooing. A ground feeder, bobbing its head as it walks. One of the few birds to drink without lifting head, same as Rock Pigeon. Parents feed their young (squab) a regurgitated liquid called crop-milk for the first few days of life. Flimsy platform nest of twigs often falls apart in a storm. Wind rushing through wing feathers in flight creates characteristic whistling sound.

winter

breeding

SUMMER

PIED-BILLED GREBE
Podilymbus podiceps

Size: 13" (33 cm)

Male: Small brown water bird with a black chin and black ring around a thick, chicken-like ivory bill. Puffy white patch under the tail. Has an unmarked brown bill during winter (September to February).

Female: same as male

Juvenile: paler than adult, with white spots and gray chest, belly and bill

Nest: floating platform; female and male build; 1 brood per year

Eggs: 5-7; bluish white without markings

Incubation: 22-24 days; female and male incubate

Fledging: 45-60 days; female and male feed young

Migration: complete, to southern states, Mexico and Central America

Food: crayfish, aquatic insects, fish

Compare: The smallest brown water bird that dives underwater for long periods of time.

Stan's Notes: This common summer resident is often seen diving for food. It slowly sinks like a submarine if disturbed. Once called Hell-diver because of the length of time it can stay submerged. Can surface far away from where it went under. Builds platform nest on a floating mat in water. Particularly sensitive to pollution. Adapted well to life on water, with short wings, lobed toes, and legs set close to the rear of body. While swimming is easy, it is very awkward on land. "Grebe" probably came from the Breton *krib*, meaning "crest," a reference to the Great Crested Grebe found in Europe.

male pg. 37

female

BUFFLEHEAD
Bucephala albeola

MIGRATION WINTER

Size:	13-15" (33-38 cm)
Female:	Brownish gray duck with dark brown head. White patch on cheek, just behind eyes.
Male:	striking black and white duck with a head that shines green purple in sunlight, large white bonnet-like patch on back of head
Juvenile:	similar to female
Nest:	cavity; female lines old woodpecker cavity; 1 brood per year
Eggs:	8-10; ivory to olive without markings
Incubation:	29-31 days; female incubates
Fledging:	50-55 days; female leads young to food
Migration:	complete, along the East coast from Maine to Florida, Mexico and Central America
Food:	aquatic insects
Compare:	Commonly confused with female Common Goldeneye (pg. 165), which lacks the white cheek patch. Slightly smaller than female Lesser Scaup (pg. 151), which has a white mark at base of bill.

Stan's Notes: Common diving duck that travels with other ducks. Usually seen during migration and winter, arriving late in August, wintering in the southern half of Maine. Most commonly found in sheltered bays and coastal harbors, it is also seen inland on rivers and lakes. Nests in old woodpecker cavities. Unlike other ducks, young remain in nests for up to two days before venturing out with their mothers. Female is very territorial and remains with the same mate for many years.

GREATER YELLOWLEGS
Tringa melanoleuca

MIGRATION

Size:	14" (36 cm)
Male:	A tall bird with bulbous head and long thin bill, slightly turned up. Gray streaking on chest and white belly. Long yellow legs.
Female:	same as male
Juvenile:	same as adult
Nest:	ground; female builds; 1 brood per year
Eggs:	3-4; off-white with brown markings
Incubation:	22-23 days; female and male incubate
Fledging:	18-20 days; male and female feed young
Migration:	complete, coastal states from New Jersey to California, Mexico and South America
Food:	small fish, aquatic insects
Compare:	Similar in size to breeding Willet (pg. 143), with a longer neck, smaller head and bright yellow legs. Greater Yellowlegs is overall a more brown bird than the breeding Willet.

Stan's Notes: A common shorebird that can be identified by the slightly upturned bill and long yellow legs. Often seen resting on one leg, its long legs carry it through deep water. Feeds by rushing forward through the water, plowing its bill or swinging it from side to side, catching small insects or fish. A skittish bird quick to give an alarm call, causing flocks to take flight. Quite often moves into the water prior to taking flight. Has a variety of "flight" notes that it gives when taking off. Nests on the ground near water on the northern tundra of Labrador and Newfoundland.

breeding

winter pg. 221

displaying

WILLET
Catoptrophorus semipalmatus

Size: 14-16" (36-40 cm)

Male: Brown breeding plumage with a brown bill and legs. White belly. Distinctive black and white wing lining pattern, seen in flight or during display.

Female: same as male

Juvenile: similar to breeding adult, more tan in color

Nest: ground; female builds; 1 brood per year

Eggs: 3-5; olive green with dark markings

Incubation: 24-28 days; male and female incubate

Fledging: unknown days; female and male feed young

Migration: complete, to southern coastal states, coastal Central and South America

Food: insects, small fish, crabs, worms, clams

Compare: Slightly larger than the Greater Yellowlegs (pg. 141), which has yellow legs.

Stan's Notes: A common summer coastal resident. Appears a rich, warm brown during breeding season and rather plain gray during winter, but it always has a striking black and white wing pattern when seen flying. Uses its black and white wing patches to display to mate. Named after the "pill-will-willet" call it gives during breeding season. Gives a "kip-kip-kip" alarm call when it takes flight. Nests along the East coast, in some western states and Canada.

GREEN-WINGED TEAL
Anas crecca

YEAR-ROUND
SUMMER

Size: 15" (38 cm)

Male: A chestnut head with a dark green patch in back of eyes extending down to the nape of neck and outlined in white. Gray body with a butter yellow tail.

Female: light brown in color with black spots, small black bill

Juvenile: same as female

Nest: ground; female builds; 1 brood per year

Eggs: 8-10; creamy white without markings

Incubation: 21-23 days; female incubates

Fledging: 32-34 days; female teaches young to feed

Migration: complete, to eastern coastal U.S., southern states, non-migrator in coastal Maine

Food: aquatic plants and insects

Compare: Male Green-winged Teal is not as colorful as the male Wood Duck (pg. 233). Female Blue-winged Teal (pg. 147) is similar in size and has a slight white mark at base of bill.

Stan's Notes: One of the smallest dabbling ducks, tipping forward in the water to glean aquatic plants and insects from the bottom of shallow freshwater ponds. Due to this behavior, it is vulnerable to ingesting spent lead shot, which can cause death. It walks well on land and thus will feed in fields and woodlands, but returns to ponds. Known for its fast and agile flight, groups spin and wheel through the air in tight formation. Green speculum is most obvious when in flight. A common summer resident in Maine, spending the winter on the coast.

145

BLUE-WINGED TEAL
Spatula discors

Size: 15-16" (38-40 cm)

Male: Small, plain-looking brown duck speckled with black. A gray head with a large white crescent-shaped mark at base of bill. Black tail with small white patch. Blue wing patch (speculum) usually only seen in flight.

Female: duller version of male, lacks facial crescent mark and white patch on tail, showing only slight white at base of bill

Juvenile: same as female

Nest: ground; female builds; 1 brood per year

Eggs: 8-11; creamy white

Incubation: 23-27 days; female incubates

Fledging: 35-44 days; female feeds young

Migration: complete, to southern states, Mexico and Central America

Food: aquatic plants, seeds, aquatic insects

Compare: Male Blue-winged has a distinct white face marking. The female is nearly half the size of female Mallard (pg. 179) and is similar to female Wood Duck (pg. 163), but lacks Wood Duck's eye-ring and crest.

Stan's Notes: A common breeding duck throughout the state. An early migrator in Maine, arriving shortly after lakes are free of ice. Builds nest some distance from water. Female performs distraction display to protect nest and young. Male leaves female near the end of incubation. Planting crops and cultivating to pond edges have caused a decline in population.

SPRUCE GROUSE
Falcipennis canadensis

YEAR-ROUND

Size: 16" (40 cm)

Male: Plump grouse, brown to almost black, with white speckles on the chest and belly. Short neck, red eyebrows (combs) and short dark tail with chestnut tip. Displaying male fans tail, leans forward and droops wings while quickly flapping wings in a short flight.

Female: overall brown grouse with small black and white barring on the chest, dark brown tail with chestnut tip

Juvenile: similar to female

Nest: ground; female builds; 1 brood per year

Eggs: 4-7; tan with brown markings

Incubation: 17-24 days; female incubates

Fledging: 8-10 days; male and female feed young

Migration: non-migrator

Food: insects, seeds, berries

Compare: Slightly larger, lighter brown Ruffed Grouse (pg. 159) has a tuft of feathers on head and tail that is not as dark as Spruce Grouse's.

Stan's Notes: Well known for being semi-tame and approachable. In winter it is often seen in groups along roads, where snow isn't as deep and small rocks can be eaten to aid in digestion. Prefers open coniferous forest. Roosts in trees. The females are territorial against other females. Cryptic coloring of female allows her to blend in with surroundings. Often freezes when danger approaches, hence its other common name, Fool Hen.

male pg. 39

female

MIGRATION

LESSER SCAUP
Aythya affinis

Size: 16-17" (40-43 cm)

Female: Overall brown duck with dull white patch at base of light gray bill. Yellow eyes.

Male: white and gray, the chest and head appear nearly black but head appears purple with green highlights in direct sun, yellow eyes

Juvenile: same as female

Nest: ground; female builds; 1 brood per year

Eggs: 8-14; olive buff without markings

Incubation: 22-28 days; female incubates

Fledging: 45-50 days; female teaches young to feed

Migration: complete, southern states, Mexico, Central America and northern South America

Food: aquatic plants and insects

Compare: Similar size as the female Ring-necked Duck (pg. 157), but lacking the white ring around the bill. Look for the white patch at base of bill to help identify the female Lesser Scaup. Male Blue-winged Teal (pg. 147) is smaller, with crescent-shaped white mark near bill.

Stan's Notes: Common migrator in Maine. This duck completely submerges itself to feed on the bottom of lakes, unlike dabbling ducks which only tip forward to reach the bottom. Often seen in large flocks on lakes, ponds and sewage lagoons during migration. When seen in flight, note the bold white stripe under the wings. An interesting baby-sitting arrangement in which groups of young are tended by one to three adult females. Prefers fresh water, but can be seen along the coast. Doesn't breed in Maine.

soaring

BROAD-WINGED HAWK
Buteo platypterus

SUMMER

Size: 14-19" (36-48 cm); up to 3-foot wingspan

Male: A hawk slightly smaller than the American Crow, the Broad-winged has a brown back and rusty red barring on the chest. Tail has two or three wide black-and-white bands. White under the wings with black "finger-tips," as seen in flight.

Female: same as male

Juvenile: tail bands narrower and more numerous, a brown-streaked chest and belly

Nest: platform; female and male build, but female finishes; 1 brood per year

Eggs: 2-3; off-white with brown markings

Incubation: 28-32 days; female incubates, male feeds female during incubation

Fledging: 34-40 days; female and male feed young

Migration: complete, to Central and South America

Food: small birds, small mammals, snakes, frogs, toads, large insects

Compare: Similar in size to Cooper's Hawk (pg. 223), but with a wider, shorter tail. Larger than Sharp-shinned Hawk (pg. 217). Look for the alternating black-and-white tail bands.

Stan's Notes: A very common woodland hawk in Maine. Can be seen in large groups (kettles) migrating early in fall. Spends most of its time hunting small birds, snakes and frogs in dense woods. Short, round wings propel it through dense woodlands. Screams its call repetitively when intruders are near the nest.

soaring

RED-SHOULDERED HAWK
Buteo lineatus

Size: 15-19" (38-48 cm); up to 3½-foot wingspan

Male: Reddish (cinnamon) head, shoulders, chest and belly. Wings and back are dark brown with white spots. Long tail with thin white bands and wide black bands. Obvious red wing linings, seen in flight.

Female: same as male

Juvenile: similar to adult, lacks the cinnamon color, has a white chest with dark spots

Nest: platform; female and male build; 1 brood per year

Eggs: 2-4; white with dark markings

Incubation: 27-29 days; female and male incubate

Fledging: 39-45 days; female and male feed young

Migration: complete, to southern states

Food: reptiles, amphibians, large insects, birds

Compare: Sharp-shinned Hawk (pg. 217) is smaller and lacks Red-shouldered's reddish head and belly. The Red-tailed Hawk (pg. 167) is larger and has a white breast.

Stan's Notes: Common woodland hawk in Maine. Prefers to hunt along edges of forests, spotting snakes, frogs, insects, an occasional small bird and other prey as it perches. Often seen flapping with an alternating gliding pattern. Very vocal hawk with a distinct scream. Mates when 2 to 3 years old. Stays in same territory for many years. Starts building nest in March to April. Young leave the nest by June to July.

male pg. 41

female

RING-NECKED DUCK
Aythya collaris

MIGRATION
SUMMER

Size: 17" (43 cm)

Female: Mainly brown back with light brown sides, a gray face and dark brown crown. White eye-ring extends into a line behind eyes. A white ring around bill. Top of head peaked.

Male: black head, breast and back, sides are gray to nearly white, bold white ring around bill and a second ring at the base of bill, top of head peaked

Juvenile: similar to female

Nest: ground; female builds; 1 brood per year

Eggs: 8-10; olive gray to brown without markings

Incubation: 26-27 days; female incubates

Fledging: 49-56 days; female teaches young to feed

Migration: complete, to southern states, West Indies, Mexico and Central America

Food: aquatic plants and insects

Compare: Female Lesser Scaup (pg. 151) is similar in size. Look for female Ring-necked's white ring around the bill.

Stan's Notes: A common breeding duck in Maine. Usually is seen in larger freshwater lakes rather than saltwater marshes. A diving duck, watch for it to dive underwater to forage for food. Takes to flight by springing up off water. Named "Ring-necked" because of the cinnamon-colored collar (nearly impossible to see in the field). Also known as Ring-billed Duck due to obvious white ring on bill.

RUFFED GROUSE
Bonasa umbellus

YEAR-ROUND

Size: 16-19" (40-48 cm)

Male: Brown chicken-like bird with long squared tail. Wide black band near tip of tail. Is able to fan tail like a turkey. Tuft of feathers on the head stands like a crown. Black ruffs on sides of neck.

Female: same as male, but less obvious neck ruffs

Juvenile: same as female

Nest: ground; female builds; 1 brood per year

Eggs: 9-12; tan with light brown markings

Incubation: 23-24 days; female incubates

Fledging: 10-12 days; female leads young to food

Migration: non-migrator

Food: seeds, insects, fruit, leaf buds

Compare: Slightly larger and lighter brown than the Spruce Grouse (pg. 149), which has a darker tail. Look for feathered tuft on head and black neck ruffs.

Stan's Notes: A common bird of deep woods. Often seen in aspen or other trees, feeding on leaf buds. In the more northern climates, grows bristles on its feet during the winter to serve as snowshoes. When there is enough snow, it will dive into a snowbank to roost at night. In spring, male raises crest (tuft), fans tail feathers, and stands on logs and drums with wings to attract females. Drumming sound comes from cupped wings moving air, not pounding on chest or log. Female will perform distraction display to protect young. Two color morphs, red and gray, most apparent in the tail. Black ruffs around the neck gave rise to its common name.

male pg. 43

female

HOODED MERGANSER
Lophodytes cucullatus

YEAR-ROUND
SUMMER

Size: 16-19" (40-48 cm)

Female: Sleek brown and rust bird with a red head. Ragged "hair" on back of head. Long, thin brown bill.

Male: same size and shape as female, but black back and rust sides, crest "hood" raises to reveal large white patch, long black bill

Juvenile: similar to female

Nest: cavity; female lines old woodpecker hole; 1 brood per year

Eggs: 10-12; white without markings

Incubation: 32-33 days; female incubates

Fledging: 71 days; female feeds young

Migration: complete, to coastal states and Mexico

Food: small fish, aquatic insects

Compare: Very similar to, but smaller than, the female Red-breasted Merganser (pg. 175), which has a larger, lighter-colored bill. Larger than female Lesser Scaup (pg. 151), which has a dull white patch at base of bill.

Stan's Notes: A small diving bird of shallow-water ponds, sloughs, lakes and rivers. It is a summer breeding duck in Maine, rarely seen away from wooded areas, where it nests in natural cavities or nest boxes. Female will "dump" eggs into other Hooded Merganser nests, resulting in 20 to 25 eggs in some nests. Frequently associated with Wood Ducks. Has been known to share a nest cavity with a Wood Duck, sitting side by side. Male Hooded Merganser can voluntarily raise and lower its crest to show off the large white head patch.

male pg. 233

female

WOOD DUCK
Aix sponsa

SUMMER

Size: 17-20" (43-50 cm)

Female: A small brown dabbling duck. Bright white eye-ring and a not-so-obvious crest. A blue patch on wing is often hidden.

Male: highly ornamented with a green head and crest patterned with white and black, rusty chest, white belly and red eyes

Juvenile: same as female

Nest: cavity; female lines old woodpecker cavity; 1 brood per year

Eggs: 10-15; creamy white without markings

Incubation: 28-36 days; female incubates

Fledging: 56-68 days; female teaches young to feed

Migration: complete, to southern states

Food: aquatic insects, plants, seeds

Compare: Smaller than the female Mallard (pg. 179) and similar to the female Blue-winged Teal (pg. 147). Mallard and Teal lack the female Duck's bright white eye-ring and crest.

Stan's Notes: A common duck of quiet, shallow backwater ponds. Nests in old woodpecker holes or in nest boxes. Often seen flying deep in forest or perched high on tree branches. Female takes flight with loud squealing call and enters nest cavity from full flight. Will lay eggs in a neighboring female nest (egg dumping), resulting in some clutches in excess of 20 eggs. Young stay in nest cavity only 24 hours after hatching, then jump from up to 30 feet (9 m) to the ground or water to follow their mother, never returning to the nest.

female

male pg. 47

YEAR-ROUND
SUMMER
WINTER

Size: 18½-20" (47-50 cm)

Female: A brown and gray duck with a large dark brown head and gray body. White collar. Bright golden eyes. Yellow-tipped dark bill.

Male: mostly white duck with a black back and a large, puffy green head, large white spot in front of each bright golden eye, dark bill

Juvenile: same as female, but has a dark bill

Nest: cavity; female lines old woodpecker cavity; 1 brood per year

Eggs: 8-10; light green without markings

Incubation: 28-32 days; female incubates

Fledging: 56-59 days; female leads young to food

Migration: complete, to southern coastal states, partial to non-migrator in southern half of Maine

Food: aquatic plants, insects

Compare: Similar to, but larger than, the brown and white female Lesser Scaup (pg. 151). Look for female Goldeneye's dark brown head and white collar.

Stan's Notes: Known for its loud whistling, produced by its wings in flight. Moves to southern and coastal Maine during winter. In late winter and early spring, male often attracts female through elaborate displays, throwing head backward while uttering a single raspy note. Female will lay eggs in other goldeneye nests, which results in some mothers incubating up to 30 eggs. Received the common name from its obvious bright golden eyes.

soaring

RED-TAILED HAWK
Buteo jamaicensis

YEAR-ROUND
SUMMER

Size: 19-25" (48-63 cm); up to 4-foot wingspan

Male: Large hawk with amazing variety of colors from bird to bird, from chocolate brown to nearly all white. Often brown with a white breast and a distinctive brown belly band. Rust red tail usually only seen from above. Underside of wing is white with small dark patch on leading edge near shoulder.

Female: same as male, only slightly larger

Juvenile: similar to adults, lacking the red tail, has a speckled chest and light eyes

Nest: platform; male and female build; 1 brood per year

Eggs: 2-3; white without markings or sometimes marked with brown

Incubation: 30-35 days; female and male incubate

Fledging: 45-46 days; male and female feed young

Migration: non-migrator to partial migrator

Food: mice, birds, snakes, insects, mammals

Compare: Red-shouldered Hawk (pg. 155) and Sharp-shinned Hawk (pg. 217) are much smaller.

Stan's Notes: A common hawk of open country and in cities in the state, often seen perched on freeway light posts, fences and trees. Look for it circling above open fields and roadsides, searching for prey. Their large stick nests are commonly seen along roads in large trees. Nests are lined with finer material such as evergreen needles. Will return to the same nest site each year. Doesn't develop red tail until second year.

YEAR-ROUND

BARRED OWL
Strix varia

Size: 20-24" (50-60 cm); up to 3½-foot wingspan

Male: A chunky brown and gray owl with a large head and dark brown eyes. Dark horizontal barring on upper chest. Vertical streaks on lower chest and belly. Yellow bill and feet.

Female: same as male, only slightly larger

Juvenile: light gray with a black face

Nest: cavity; does not add any nesting material; 1 brood per year

Eggs: 2-3; white without markings

Incubation: 28-33 days; female incubates

Fledging: 42-44 days; female and male feed young

Migration: non-migrator

Food: mammals, birds, fish, reptiles, amphibians

Compare: Barred Owl lacks the "horns" of the Great Horned Owl (pg. 171). Northern Saw-whet Owl (pg. 117) is less than half the size of Barred Owl and has yellow eyes.

Stan's Notes: A very common owl that can often be seen hunting in daytime, perching and watching for mice, birds and other prey. One of the few owls to take fish out of a lake. Prefers dense deciduous woodland with sparse undergrowth. Can be attracted with a simple nest box with a large opening, attached to a tree. The young will stay with their parents for up to four months after fledging. Often sounds like a dog barking just before giving an eight-hoot call that sounds like, "Who-cooks-for-you? Who-cooks-for-you?" The Great Horned Owl sounds like, "Hoo-hoo-hoo-hoooo!"

GREAT HORNED OWL
Bubo virginianus

YEAR-ROUND

Size: 20-25" (50-63 cm); up to 3½-foot wingspan

Male: Robust brown "horned" owl. Bright yellow eyes and V-shaped white throat resembling a necklace. Horizontal barring on the chest.

Female: same as male, only slightly larger

Juvenile: similar to adults, lacking ear tufts

Nest: no nest; takes over the nests of crows, Great Blue Herons and hawks, or will use partial cavities, stumps or broken-off trees; 1 brood per year

Eggs: 2; white without markings

Incubation: 26-30 days; female incubates

Fledging: 30-35 days; male and female feed young

Migration: non-migrator

Food: mammals, birds (ducks), snakes, insects

Compare: Barred Owl (pg. 169) has dark eyes and no "horns." Over twice the size of Northern Saw-whet Owl (pg. 117).

Stan's Notes: The largest owl in the state and one of the earliest nesting birds in Maine, laying eggs in January and February. Has excellent hearing; able to hear a mouse moving beneath a foot of snow. "Ears" are actually tufts of feathers (horns) and have nothing to do with hearing. Not able to turn head all the way around. Wing feathers are ragged on the end, resulting in a silent flight. Eyelids close from the top down, like humans. Fearless, it is one of the few animals that will kill skunks and porcupines. Because of this, it is sometimes called Flying Tiger.

male

female

AMERICAN BLACK DUCK
Anas rubripes

Size: 23" (58 cm)

Male: Overall dark brown, sometimes appearing nearly black. Neck and head are lighter in color. Yellow bill and orange legs. When in flight, white wing linings contrast sharply with dark wings. Violet patch (speculum) on wing is bordered in black.

Female: same as male, except bill is dull green with black flecks

Juvenile: same as female

Nest: ground; female builds; 1 brood per year

Eggs: 8-10; creamy white to greenish buff

Incubation: 26-29 days; female incubates

Fledging: 16-17 days; female teaches young to feed

Migration: complete, to southern states, non-migrator in southern half of Maine

Food: aquatic plants, seeds

Compare: Both the male and female American Black Ducks are very similar to female Mallard (pg. 179), but the female Mallard has a blue wing patch (speculum) bordered by white, and an orange bill.

Stan's Notes: Hybridizes (mates) with Mallards, producing a bird lacking the brilliant colors of the male Mallard. Formerly one of the most abundant ducks breeding in the U.S. Now Mallards are more common. The female builds a nest in grass tall enough to conceal herself. Male leaves female while she is incubating the eggs. Young leave the nest one to three hours after hatching.

male pg. 235

female

RED-BREASTED MERGANSER
Mergus serrator

YEAR-ROUND
MIGRATION
SUMMER
WINTER

Size: 23" (58 cm)

Female: Overall brown-to-gray duck with a shaggy reddish head and crest. Long orange bill.

Male: shaggy green head and crest, a prominent white collar, rusty breast, black and white body, long orange bill

Juvenile: similar to female

Nest: ground; female builds; 1 brood per year

Eggs: 5-10; olive green without markings

Incubation: 29-30 days; female incubates

Fledging: 55-65 days; female feeds young

Migration: complete, to coastal Maine and southern coastal states, Central America

Food: fish, aquatic insects

Compare: Very similar to, but larger than, the female Hooded Merganser (pg. 161), which has a smaller, darker bill than the bill of female Red-breasted Merganser.

Stan's Notes: A very fast flier, often seen flying low and fast across water. Needs a long take-off run to get airborne. Serrated bill helps it catch slippery fish. Doesn't breed before 2 years of age. The male abandons female just after eggs are laid. Females often share a nest. Breeds in Alaska, northern Canada and inland Maine, wintering on the coast.

male
pg. 225

female

soaring

NORTHERN HARRIER
Circus hudsonius

YEAR-ROUND
SUMMER

Size: 24" (60 cm); up to 4-foot wingspan

Female: A slim, low-flying hawk. Dark brown back with brown-streaked breast and belly. Large white rump patch and narrow black bands across tail. Tips of wings black. Yellow eyes.

Male: silver gray with large white rump patch and white belly, faint narrow bands across tail, tips of wings black, yellow eyes

Juvenile: similar to female, with an orange breast

Nest: ground; female and male construct; 1 brood per year

Eggs: 4-8; bluish white without markings

Incubation: 31-32 days; female incubates

Fledging: 30-35 days; male and female feed young

Migration: complete, to southern states, Mexico and Central America; winters in coastal Maine

Food: mice, snakes, insects, small birds

Compare: Slimmer than Red-tailed Hawk (pg. 167). Look for black bands on tail and a white rump patch.

Stan's Notes: One of the easiest hawks to identify. Harriers glide just above ground, following contours of the land while searching for prey. Holds its wings just above the horizontal position, tilting back and forth in the wind, similar to Turkey Vultures. Formerly called Marsh Hawk due to its habit of hunting over marshes. Feeds on the ground. Will perch on the ground to preen and rest. At any age, has a distinctive owl-like face disk.

male pg. 239

female

MALLARD
Anas platyrhynchos

YEAR-ROUND

Size:	27-28" (69-71 cm)
Female:	Brown duck with an orange and black bill and blue and white wing mark (speculum).
Male:	large, bulbous green head, white necklace, rust brown or chestnut chest, combination of gray and white on the sides, yellow bill, orange legs and feet
Juvenile:	same as female, but with a yellow bill
Nest:	ground; female builds; 1 brood per year
Eggs:	7-10; greenish to whitish, unmarked
Incubation:	26-30 days; female incubates
Fledging:	42-52 days; female leads young to food
Migration:	complete, to southern states, non-migrator in parts of Maine
Food:	seeds, plants, aquatic insects; will come to ground feeders offering corn
Compare:	The female Blue-winged Teal (pg. 147) is nearly half the size of the female Mallard. The female Wood Duck (pg. 163) is also smaller and has a white eye-ring.

Stan's Notes: A familiar duck of lakes and ponds, it's considered a type of dabbling duck, tipping forward in shallow water to feed on aquatic plants on the bottom. The name "Mallard" comes from the Latin *masculus*, meaning "male," referring to the habit of males not taking part in raising ducklings. Both female and male have white tails and white underwings. Black central tail feathers of male curl upward. Will return to place of birth.

displaying male

non-displaying

female

WILD TURKEY
Meleagris gallopavo

YEAR-ROUND

Size:	36-48" (90-120 cm)
Male:	Large, plump brown and bronze bird with striking blue and red bare head. Fan tail and long, straight black beard in center of chest. Spurs on legs.
Female:	thinner and less striking than male, usually lacking breast beard
Juvenile:	same as adult of the same sex
Nest:	ground; female builds; 1 brood per year
Eggs:	10-12; buff white with dull brown markings
Incubation:	27-28 days; female incubates
Fledging:	6-10 days; female leads young to food
Migration:	non-migrator
Food:	insects, seeds, fruit
Compare:	This bird is quite distinctive and unlikely to be confused with others.

Stan's Notes: The largest game bird in Maine, this is the bird from which the domestic turkey was bred. Once eliminated from many eastern states due to market hunting and loss of habitat, they were reintroduced widely in the 1960s to 1980s. Now populations are stable. Strong fliers, they can approach 60 miles (97 km) per hour. Can fly straight up, then away. Eyesight is three times better than in humans. Hearing is also excellent; able to hear competing males up to a mile away. Males hold "harems" of up to 20 females. Males are known as toms, females are hens and young are called poults. At night, they roost in trees.

RUBY-CROWNED KINGLET
Regulus calendula

MIGRATION
SUMMER

Size: 4" (10 cm)

Male: Small, teardrop-shaped green-to-gray bird. Two white wing bars. Hidden ruby-colored crown. White eye-ring.

Female: same as male, but lacking the ruby crown

Juvenile: same as female

Nest: pendulous; female builds; 1 brood per year

Eggs: 4-5; white with brown markings

Incubation: 11-12 days; female incubates

Fledging: 11-12 days; female and male feed young

Migration: complete, to southern states, Mexico and Central America

Food: insects, berries

Compare: The Golden-crowned Kinglet (pg. 185) is similar, but lacks a ruby crown. The female American Goldfinch (pg. 269) is larger, but shares the olive color and clear chest. Look for Ruby-crowned's white eye-ring.

Stan's Notes: One of the smaller birds in Maine, it takes a quick eye to see the male's ruby crown. A summer resident, but is most commonly seen during spring and autumn migrations. Look for it flitting around thick shrubs low to the ground. Female builds an unusual pendulous (sac-like) nest. Intricately woven and decorated on the outside with colored lichens and mosses stuck together with spider webs, the nest is suspended from a branch overlapped by leaves, and usually hung high in a mature tree. "Kinglet" comes from the Anglo-Saxon word *cyning*, or "king," referring to the male's ruby crown, and the diminutive suffix "let," meaning "small."

GOLDEN-CROWNED KINGLET
Regulus satrapa

YEAR-ROUND

Size: 4" (10 cm)

Male: Tiny, plump green-to-gray bird. Distinctive yellow and orange patch with black border on the crown. A white eyebrow mark. Two white wing bars.

Female: same as male, but has a yellow crown with black border, lacks any orange

Juvenile: same as adults, but lacks gold on crown

Nest: pendulous; female builds; 1-2 broods a year

Eggs: 5-9; white or creamy with brown markings

Incubation: 14-15 days; female incubates

Fledging: 14-19 days; female and male feed young

Migration: complete, to southern states, Mexico and Central America, non-migrator in Maine

Food: insects, fruit, tree sap

Compare: Similar to Ruby-crowned Kinglet (pg. 183), but Golden-crowned has an obvious crown. Smaller than the female American Goldfinch (pg. 269), which lacks any crown marking.

Stan's Notes: Common year-round resident in the state, but might be more frequently seen during migration when flocks from farther north move through Maine. It is often seen in flocks that include chickadees, nuthatches, woodpeckers, Brown Creepers and Ruby-crowned Kinglets. Habit of flicking its wings when moving around. Unusual hanging nest is often made of moss, lichens and spider webs, and lined with bark and feathers. Can have so many eggs in its small nest that eggs are in two layers. Drinks tree sap and feeds by gleaning insects from trees. Can be very tame and approachable.

RED-BREASTED NUTHATCH
Sitta canadensis

YEAR-ROUND

Size: 4½" (11 cm)

Male: A small gray-backed bird with a black cap and a prominent eye line. A rust red breast and belly.

Female: gray cap, pale undersides

Juvenile: same as female

Nest: cavity; male and female excavate; 1 brood per year

Eggs: 5-6; white with red brown markings

Incubation: 11-12 days; female incubates

Fledging: 14-20 days; female and male feed young

Migration: non-migrator to irruptive; moves around in search of food

Food: insects, seeds; visits seed and suet feeders

Compare: Smaller than the White-breasted Nuthatch (pg. 191), with a red chest instead of white.

Stan's Notes: The Red-breasted Nuthatch behaves like the White-breasted Nuthatch, climbing down tree trunks headfirst. Similar to chickadees, visits seed feeders, quickly grabbing a seed and flying off to crack it open. Will wedge a seed into a crevice and pound it open with several sharp blows. The name "Nuthatch" comes from the Middle English moniker *nuthak*, referring to the bird's habit of wedging a seed into a crevice and hacking it open. Look for it in mature conifers, where it often extracts seeds from cones. Excavates a cavity or takes a vacant woodpecker hole or natural cavity and constructs a nest.

BLACK-CAPPED CHICKADEE
Poecile atricapillus

YEAR-ROUND

Size: 5" (13 cm)

Male: Familiar gray bird with black cap and throat patch. White chest. Tan belly. Small white wing marks.

Female: same as male

Juvenile: same as adult

Nest: cavity; female and male build or excavate; 1 brood per year

Eggs: 5-7; white with fine brown markings

Incubation: 11-13 days; female and male incubate

Fledging: 14-18 days; female and male feed young

Migration: non-migrator

Food: insects, seeds, fruit; comes to seed and suet feeders

Compare: Tufted Titmouse (pg. 197) is larger than the Black-capped Chickadee and has a crest.

Stan's Notes: Widespread and common bird throughout the state. It is a backyard bird that can be attracted with a simple nest box or seed feeder. Usually is the first to find a new feeder. Can be easily tamed and hand fed. Can be a common urban bird since much of its diet comes from bird feeders. Needs to feed each day in winter; consequently seen foraging for food during even the worst winter storms. Frequently seen with other birds such as nuthatches and woodpeckers. Makes its nest mostly with green moss, lining it with animal fur. Common name comes from its familiar "chika-dee-dee-dee-dee" call. It also gives a high-pitched, two-toned "fee-bee" call. Can have different calls in various regions.

WHITE-BREASTED NUTHATCH
Sitta carolinensis

YEAR-ROUND

Size: 5-6" (13-15 cm)

Male: Slate gray with a white face and belly, and black cap and nape. Long thin bill, slightly upturned. Chestnut undertail.

Female: similar to male, gray cap and nape

Juvenile: similar to female

Nest: cavity; the female and male build; 1 brood per year

Eggs: 5-7; white with brown markings

Incubation: 11-12 days; female incubates

Fledging: 13-14 days; female and male feed young

Migration: non-migrator

Food: insects, seeds; visits seed and suet feeders

Compare: Red-breasted Nuthatch (pg. 187) is smaller, with a rust red belly and a distinctive black eye line.

Stan's Notes: The nuthatch's habit of hopping headfirst down tree trunks helps it see insects and insect eggs that birds climbing up the trunk might miss. Incredible climbing agility comes from an extra-long hind toe claw or nail, nearly twice the size of the front toe claws. The name "Nuthatch" comes from the Middle English moniker *nuthak*, referring to the bird's habit of wedging a seed into a crevice and hacking it open. Often seen in mixed flocks of Brown Creepers, chickadees and Downy Woodpeckers. This year-round resident is abundant throughout Maine. Will use a nest box. Mated pairs stay together all year long, defending small territories. Listen for its characteristic spring call, "whi-whi-whi-whi," given during February and March.

male

female

YELLOW-RUMPED WARBLER
Setophaga coronata

YEAR-ROUND
SUMMER

Size: 5-6" (13-15 cm)

Male: Slate gray bird with black streaks on breast. Yellow patch on the head, flanks and rump. White chin and belly. Two white wing bars.

Female: duller than male, but same yellow patches

Juvenile: similar to female

Nest: cup; female builds; 2 broods per year

Eggs: 4-5; white with brown markings

Incubation: 12-13 days; female incubates

Fledging: 10-12 days; female and male feed young

Migration: complete, to southern states, Mexico and Central America; winters in coastal Maine

Food: insects, berries; rarely comes to suet feeders

Compare: Male Yellow Warbler (pg. 275) is all yellow with orange streaks on chest. Palm Warbler (pg. 279) has a yellow throat and chestnut crown. Common Yellowthroat (pg. 271) has a yellow breast. Look for a combination of yellow patches on the Yellow-rumped's head, flanks and rump.

Stan's Notes: One of the most common warblers in Maine. Male molts to a dull color in winter similar to female, retaining yellow patches. Sometimes called Butter-butts due to the yellow patch on rump. Formerly known as Audubon's or Myrtle Warbler. Familiar call is a robust "chip." Nests in coniferous and aspen forests.

female
pg. 89

male

DARK-EYED JUNCO
Junco hyemalis

YEAR-ROUND

Size: 5½" (14 cm)

Male: Round, dark-eyed bird with a slate gray-to-charcoal chest, head and back. White belly. Pink bill. Since the outermost tail feathers are white, tail appears as a white V in flight.

Female: same as male, only tan-to-brown color

Juvenile: similar to female, but has a streaked breast and head

Nest: cup; female and male construct; 2 broods per year

Eggs: 3-5; white with reddish brown markings

Incubation: 12-13 days; female incubates

Fledging: 10-13 days; male and female feed young

Migration: complete, across the United States, non-migrator in Maine

Food: seeds, insects; will come to seed feeders

Compare: Rarely confused with any other bird. Small flocks feed under bird feeders in winter.

Stan's Notes: A year-round resident in Maine, but usually is more commonly seen during the winter. Usually seen on the ground in small flocks. Migrates from Canada to Maine and beyond, swelling resident populations. Females tend to migrate farther south than males. It adheres to a rigid social hierarchy, with dominant birds chasing the less dominant birds. Look for white outer tail feathers flashing while in flight. Most comfortable on the ground, juncos will use both feet to "double-scratch," exposing seeds and insects. Consumes many weed seeds. Several junco species have now been combined into one, simply called Dark-eyed Junco.

195

TUFTED TITMOUSE
Baeolophus bicolor

YEAR-ROUND

Size: 6" (15 cm)

Male: Slate gray bird with a white chest and belly. Pointed crest. Flanks are washed in a rusty brown. Gray legs and dark eyes.

Female: same as male

Juvenile: same as adult

Nest: cavity; female lines old woodpecker hole; 2 broods per year

Eggs: 5-7; white with brown markings

Incubation: 13-14 days; female incubates

Fledging: 15-18 days; female and male feed young

Migration: non-migrator

Food: insects, seeds, fruit; will come to seed and suet feeders

Compare: Closely related to Black-capped Chickadee (pg. 189), but Titmouse is slightly larger and has a crest. Similar in size and color to the White-breasted Nuthatch (pg. 191), but Nuthatch lacks a crest.

Stan's Notes: A common feeder bird, it can be attracted with black oil sunflower seeds. Well known for its quickly repeated "peter-peter-peter" call. Prefix "Tit" comes from a Scandinavian word meaning "little." Suffix "mouse" is derived from the Old English word *mase*, meaning "bird." Simply translated, it is a "small bird." Notorious for pulling hair from sleeping dogs, cats and squirrels to line their nests. Attracted with nest boxes. Usually seen only one or two at a time. Male feeds female during courtship and nesting.

EASTERN PHOEBE
Sayornis phoebe

SUMMER

Size: 7" (18 cm)

Male: Gray bird with dark wings, light olive green belly and a thin dark bill.

Female: same as male

Juvenile: same as adult

Nest: cup; female builds; 2 broods per year

Eggs: 4-5; white without markings

Incubation: 15-16 days; female incubates

Fledging: 15-16 days; male and female feed young

Migration: complete, to southern states and Mexico

Food: insects

Compare: Like most other olive gray birds, it is hard to distinguish identifying markings. Eastern Phoebe lacks any white eye-ring. Easier to identify by well-enunciated song, "fee-bee," or characteristic of hawking for insects.

Stan's Notes: A sparrow-sized bird often seen on the end of a dead branch. It sits in wait for a passing insect, flies out to catch it, then returns to the same branch, a process called hawking. Has a habit of pumping its tail up and down and spreading it when perched. Will build its nest under the eaves of a house, under a bridge or in culverts. Nest is constructed with mud, grass and moss, and lined with hair (and sometimes feathers). The name is derived from its characteristic song, "fee-bee," which is repeated over and over from the tops of dead branches.

GREAT CRESTED FLYCATCHER
Myiarchus crinitus

SUMMER

Size: 8" (20 cm)

Male: Gray head with prominent crest. Gray back and throat with bright yellow belly, yellow extending under reddish brown tail. Lower bill is yellow at base.

Female: same as male

Juvenile: same as adult

Nest: cavity; the female and male build; 1 brood per year

Eggs: 4-6; white or buff with brown markings

Incubation: 13-15 days; female incubates

Fledging: 14-21 days; female and male feed young

Migration: complete, to Mexico and Central America

Food: insects, fruit

Compare: The Eastern Kingbird (pg. 203) has a white band across the tail. Similar to the Eastern Phoebe (pg. 199), but the Flycatcher has an obvious crest and yellow belly.

Stan's Notes: Breeds throughout Maine. Common in almost any wooded area, it lives high up in trees, rarely coming to the ground. Often heard before seen. The first part of its common name refers to the set of extra long feathers on the top of its head (crest), which the bird raises when alert or agitated, similar to Northern Cardinals. Feeds by gleaning insects from tree leaves. Nests in old woodpecker holes, but can be attracted to a nest box placed high in a tree with a 1½- to 2½-inch (4 to 6 cm) entrance hole. Often stuffs its nest with a collection of fur, feathers, string and snakeskins.

EASTERN KINGBIRD
Tyrannus tyrannus

SUMMER

Size: 8" (20 cm)

Male: Mostly black gray bird with white belly and chin. Black head and tail with a distinctive white band across the end of the tail. Has a concealed red crown that is rarely seen.

Female: same as male

Juvenile: same as adult

Nest: cup; male and female build; 1 brood a year

Eggs: 3-4; white with brown markings

Incubation: 16-18 days; female incubates

Fledging: 16-18 days; female and male feed young

Migration: complete, to Mexico, Central America and South America

Food: insects, fruit

Compare: Rarely confused with other birds. Medium-sized bird, smaller than American Robin (pg. 211). Look for the white band along the end of the tail to identify.

Stan's Notes: Common bird throughout Maine in open fields and prairies. Fall migration begins in late August and early September, with groups of up to 20 individuals migrating together. Returns to mating ground in spring, where the male and female defend their territory. Acting unafraid of other birds and chasing the larger ones, it is perceived as having an attitude. Its bold behavior gave rise to the common name, King. Perches on tall branches, watching for insects. After flying out to catch them, returns to the same perch, a technique called hawking.

GRAY CATBIRD
Dumetella carolinensis

SUMMER

Size: 9" (22.5 cm)

Male: Handsome slate gray bird with black crown and a long, thin black bill. Often seen with its tail lifted, exposing a chestnut-colored patch under tail.

Female: same as male

Juvenile: same as adult

Nest: cup; female and male build; 2 broods a year

Eggs: 4-6; blue green without markings

Incubation: 12-13 days; female incubates

Fledging: 10-11 days; female and male feed young

Migration: complete, to southern states

Food: insects, fruit

Compare: Larger than Eastern Phoebe (pg. 199), it lacks the Phoebe's olive belly. Similar size as Eastern Kingbird (pg. 203), but it lacks the Kingbird's white belly and white tail band.

Stan's Notes: Returns to Maine by the last week of April. Secretive bird that the Chippewa Indians named Bird That Cries With Grief due to its raspy call. The call sounds like the mewing of a house cat, hence the common name. Frequently mimics other birds and rarely repeats the same phrases. More often heard than seen. Nests only in thick shrubs, quickly flying back into shrubs if approached. If a cowbird introduces an egg into a catbird nest, the catbird will quickly break it, then eject it.

male pg. 11

female

RUSTY BLACKBIRD
Euphagus carolinus

MIGRATION
SUMMER

Size: 9" (22.5 cm)

Female: Overall gray bird. Rusty edges of feathers. Yellow eyes. Has a short, pointed thin bill. Non-breeding is much browner with a gray rump and black patch around each eye.

Male: glossy black in color with highlights of blue and purple, bright yellow eyes, has a short, pointed thin bill, non-breeding plumage is more of a rusty brown than glossy black

Juvenile: similar to female

Nest: cup; female builds; 1-2 broods per year

Eggs: 4-5; bluish with brown markings

Incubation: 12-14 days; female incubates

Fledging: 11-13 days; male and female feed young

Migration: complete, to southeastern states

Food: insects, seeds

Compare: Female Red-winged Blackbird (pg. 121) is slightly smaller and heavily streaked, with prominent white eyebrows. Female Brown-headed Cowbird (pg. 111) is uniform light brown in color, with dark eyes.

Stan's Notes: This bird nests across the northern half of Maine in small loose colonies, often preferring more wooded, swampy areas. Male feeds female while she incubates. Gathers in large groups and with other blackbirds to migrate each autumn. When in flight, end of tail often appears squared.

male pg. 253

female

PINE GROSBEAK
Pinicola enucleator

YEAR-ROUND
WINTER

Size: 9" (22.5 cm)

Female: A plump gray winter finch with a long dark tail. Dark wings with two white wing bars. Head and rump tinged dull yellow. Short, stubby, pointed dark bill.

Male: overall rosy red and gray

Juvenile: female is similar to adult female, male has a touch of red on head and rump

Nest: cup; female builds; 1 brood per year

Eggs: 4-5; bluish green without markings

Incubation: 13-15 days; female incubates

Fledging: 13-20 days; female and male feed young

Migration: non-migrator to irruptive; moves around to find food

Food: seeds, fruit, insects; will come to feeders

Compare: Much larger than the female Purple Finch (pg. 95) and female House Finch (pg. 83).

Stan's Notes: Very tame and approachable bird. Often seen along roads or on the ground, eating tiny grains of sand and dirt to aid digestion. A seed eater that favors coniferous woods, rarely moving out of coniferous regions during summer. Frequently seen bathing in fluffy snow. Flies with a typical finch-like undulating pattern while calling a soft whistle. During breeding season, both male and female develop a pouch in the bottom of the mouth (buccal pouch) to transport seeds to young.

male

female

YEAR-ROUND
SUMMER

AMERICAN ROBIN
Turdus migratorius

Size: 9-11" (22.5-28 cm)

Male: A familiar gray bird with a rusty red breast, and nearly black head and tail. White chin with black streaks. White eye-ring.

Female: similar to male, but with a gray head and a duller breast

Juvenile: similar to female, but has a speckled breast and brown back

Nest: cup; female builds with help from the male; 2-3 broods per year

Eggs: 4-7; pale blue without markings

Incubation: 12-14 days; female incubates

Fledging: 14-16 days; female and male feed young

Migration: complete, to southern states, non-migrator in southern half of Maine

Food: insects, fruit, berries, worms

Compare: Familiar bird to all.

Stan's Notes: Although complete migrators in northern states, the robin can be a year-round resident in portions of southern Maine. Some will not migrate, spending the winter in low swampy areas, feeding on leftover berries and insect eggs. Can be heard singing all night long in the spring. Most don't realize how easy it is to tell the difference between the male and female. Compare the male's dark, nearly black head and brick red breast with the female's gray head and dull red breast. Robins are not listening for worms when they cock their heads to one side. They are looking with eyes placed far back on the sides of their heads. A very territorial bird. Often seen fighting its own reflection in windows.

displaying

NORTHERN MOCKINGBIRD
Mimus polyglottos

YEAR-ROUND

Size: 10" (25 cm)

Male: Silvery gray head and back with light gray chest and belly. White wing patches, seen in flight or during display. Tail mostly black with white outer tail feathers. Black bill.

Female: same as male

Juvenile: dull gray overall, heavily streaked chest and gray bill

Nest: cup; female and male build; 2 broods per year, sometimes more

Eggs: 3-5; blue green with brown markings

Incubation: 12-13 days; female incubates

Fledging: 11-13 days; female and male feed young

Migration: partial migrator to non-migrator in Maine

Food: insects, fruit

Compare: The Gray Catbird (pg. 205) is slate gray and lacks wing patches. Look for Mockingbird to spread its wings, flash its white wing patches and wag its tail from side to side.

Stan's Notes: Very animated, male and female perform elaborate mating dances by facing each other, heads and tails erect. They run toward each other, flashing white wing patches, and then retreat to nearby cover. Thought to also flash wing patches to scare up insects when hunting. Known to imitate other birds (vocal mimicry), hence its common name. Young males often sing at night.

CANADA JAY
Perisoreus canadensis

YEAR-ROUND

Size: 11½" (29 cm)

Male: A large gray bird with black nape and white chest. Short black bill and dark eyes. White patch on forehead.

Female: same as male

Juvenile: sooty gray with a faint white whisker mark

Nest: cup; male and female build; 1 brood a year

Eggs: 3-4; gray white, finely marked to unmarked

Incubation: 16-18 days; female incubates

Fledging: 14-15 days; male and female feed young

Migration: non-migrator

Food: insects, seeds, fruit, nuts; visits seed feeders

Compare: Similar size as Blue Jay (pg. 67), but lacks the Blue Jay's crest and blue coloring.

Stan's Notes: A bird of coniferous woods. Known as Camp Robber because it rummages through camps looking for food scraps. Also called Whisky Jack or Gray Jay. Easily tamed, this bird will fly to your hand if offered raisins or nuts. Will eat just about anything. Also stores extra food for winter, balling it together in a sticky mass, placing it on a tree branch, often concealing it with lichen or bark. Travels around in small family units of three to five, making good companions for campers and canoeists. Reminds some people of an overgrown chickadee.

soaring

juvenile

SHARP-SHINNED HAWK
Accipiter striatus

YEAR-ROUND
SUMMER

Size: 10-14" (25-36 cm); up to 2-foot wingspan

Male: Small woodland hawk with gray back and head, and rusty red breast. Long tail with several dark tail bands, widest band at end of squared-off tail. Red eyes.

Female: same as male, only larger

Juvenile: same size as adults, with a brown back and heavily streaked breast, yellow eyes

Nest: platform; female builds; 1 brood per year

Eggs: 4-5; white with brown markings

Incubation: 32-35 days; female incubates

Fledging: 24-27 days; female and male feed young

Migration: complete, southern states, Mexico, Central America, non-migrator in most of Maine

Food: birds, small mammals

Compare: Nearly identical to Cooper's Hawk (pg. 223), only smaller. Look for the Sharp-shinned's squared tail, compared with the rounded tail of the Cooper's. Red-shouldered Hawk (pg. 155) is larger and lacks a gray back.

Stan's Notes: Common hawk of backyards and woodlands, often seen swooping in on birds visiting feeders. Short rounded wings and long tail allow this hawk to navigate through thick stands of trees in pursuit of prey. Common name comes from the sharp keel on the leading edge of its "shin," although it's actually below rather than above the bird's ankle on the tarsus bone of foot. The tarsus in most birds is round. In flight, head doesn't protrude as far as the head of the Cooper's Hawk.

ROCK PIGEON
Columba livia

YEAR-ROUND

Size: 13" (33 cm)

Male: No set color pattern. Gray to white, patches of iridescent greens and blues, usually with a light rump patch.

Female: same as male

Juvenile: same as adult

Nest: platform; female builds; 3-4 broods a year

Eggs: 1-2; white without markings

Incubation: 18-20 days; female and male incubate

Fledging: 25-26 days; female and male feed young

Migration: non-migrator

Food: seeds

Compare: The Mourning Dove (pg. 135) is smaller and light brown in color.

Stan's Notes: Also known as Domestic Pigeon, it was introduced to North America from Europe by the early settlers. Most common around cities and barnyards, where it scratches for seeds. One of the few birds that has a wide variety of colors, produced by years of selective breeding while in captivity. Parents feed their young a regurgitated liquid known as crop-milk for the first few days of life. One of the few birds that can drink without tilting its head back. Nests under bridges and on buildings, balconies, barns and sheds. Was once poisoned as a "nuisance city bird." Many cities now have Peregrine Falcons (not shown) that feed on Rock Pigeons, keeping their numbers in check.

**breeding
pg. 143**

displaying

winter

WILLET
Catoptrophorus semipalmatus

SUMMER

Size: 14-16" (36-40 cm)

Male: Winter plumage is gray with a gray bill and legs. White belly. A distinctive black and white wing lining pattern, seen in flight or during display.

Female: same as male

Juvenile: similar to breeding adult, more tan in color

Nest: ground; female builds; 1 brood per year

Eggs: 3-5; olive green with dark markings

Incubation: 24-28 days; male and female incubate

Fledging: unknown days; female and male feed young

Migration: complete, to southern coastal states, coastal Central and South America

Food: insects, small fish, crabs, worms, clams

Compare: Slightly larger than the Greater Yellowlegs (pg. 141), which has yellow legs.

Stan's Notes: A common summer coastal resident. Appears a rich, warm brown during breeding season and rather plain gray during winter, but it always has a striking black and white wing pattern when seen flying. Uses its black and white wing patches to display to mate. Named after the "pill-will-willet" call it gives during breeding season. Gives a "kip-kip-kip" alarm call when it takes flight. Nests along the East coast, in some western states and Canada.

soaring

juvenile

COOPER'S HAWK
Accipiter cooperii

Size: 14-20" (36-50 cm); up to 2½-foot wingspan

Male: Medium-sized hawk with short wings and long rounded tail with several black bands. Rusty breast and dark wing tips. Slate gray back. Bright yellow spot at base of gray bill (cere). Dark red eyes.

Female: similar to male, only slightly larger

Juvenile: brown back with brown streaks on breast, bright yellow eyes

Nest: platform; male and female build; 1 brood per year

Eggs: 2-4; greenish with brown markings

Incubation: 32-36 days; female and male incubate

Fledging: 28-32 days; male and female feed young

Migration: complete, to southern states, non-migrator in southern half of Maine

Food: small birds, mammals

Compare: Nearly identical to the Sharp-shinned Hawk (pg. 217), only larger, darker gray and with a rounded-off tail.

Stan's Notes: Resident hawk of woodland in Maine. In flight, look for its large head, short wings and long tail. The short stubby wings help it maneuver between trees while pursuing small birds. Will come to feeders, hunting for unaware birds. Flies with long glides followed by a few quick flaps. Known to ambush prey, it will fly into heavy brush or even run on the ground in pursuit. Nestlings have gray eyes that become bright yellow at 1 year of age and dark red later.

male

female
pg. 177

soaring

NORTHERN HARRIER
Circus hudsonius

YEAR-ROUND
SUMMER

Size: 24" (60 cm); up to 4-foot wingspan

Male: A slim, low-flying hawk. Silver gray with a large white rump patch and a white belly. Faint narrow bands across the tail. Tips of wings black. Yellow eyes.

Female: dark brown back, a brown-streaked breast and belly, large white rump patch, narrow black bands across tail, tips of wings black, yellow eyes

Juvenile: similar to female, with an orange breast

Nest: ground; female and male construct; 1 brood per year

Eggs: 4-8; bluish white without markings

Incubation: 31-32 days; female incubates

Fledging: 30-35 days; male and female feed young

Migration: complete, to southern states, Mexico and Central America; winters in coastal Maine

Food: mice, snakes, insects, small birds

Compare: Slimmer than Red-tailed Hawk (pg. 167). Look for black bands on tail and a white rump patch.

Stan's Notes: One of the easiest hawks to identify. Harriers glide just above ground, following contours of the land while searching for prey. Holds its wings just above the horizontal position, tilting back and forth in the wind, similar to Turkey Vultures. Formerly called Marsh Hawk due to its habit of hunting over marshes. Feeds on the ground. Will perch on the ground to preen and rest. At any age, has a distinctive owl-like face disk.

YEAR-ROUND
SUMMER

CANADA GOOSE
Branta canadensis

Size: 25-43" (63-109 cm)

Male: Large gray goose with black neck and head, with a white chin or cheek strap.

Female: same as male

Juvenile: same as adult

Nest: platform, on the ground; female builds; 1 brood per year

Eggs: 5-10; white without markings

Incubation: 25-30 days; female incubates

Fledging: 42-55 days; male and female teach young to feed

Migration: non-migrator to partial migrator

Food: aquatic plants, insects, seeds

Compare: Large goose that is rarely confused with any other bird.

Stan's Notes: Formerly killed off (extirpated) in many areas, it was reintroduced and is now a common year-round resident. Adapting to our changed environment very well, it now breeds in Maine. Adults mate for many years, but only start to breed in their third year. Males often act as sentinels, standing at the edge of the group, bobbing their heads up and down, becoming very aggressive to anybody approaching. Will hiss as if displaying displeasure. Adults molt primary flight feathers while raising their young, rendering family groups flightless at the same time. Several subspecies vary geographically around the U.S. Generally they are paler in color in eastern groups, darker in western. Size decreases northward, with the smallest subspecies found on the Arctic tundra.

GREAT BLUE HERON
Ardea herodias

SUMMER

Size: 42-52" (107-132 cm)

Male: Tall gray heron. Black eyebrows extend into several long plumes off the back of head. Long yellow bill. Feathers at base of neck drop down in a kind of necklace.

Female: same as male

Juvenile: same as adult, but more brown than gray, with a black crown and no plumes

Nest: platform; male and female build; 1 brood per year

Eggs: 3-5; blue green without markings

Incubation: 27-28 days; female and male incubate

Fledging: 56-60 days; male and female feed young

Migration: complete, to southern states, Mexico, and Central and South America

Food: small fish, frogs, insects, snakes

Compare: Larger in size than the all-white Great Egret (pg. 267), but similar in shape.

Stan's Notes: One of the most common herons, often barking like a dog when startled. Seen stalking small fish in shallow water. Will strike at mice, squirrels and just about anything else it might come across. Flies holding neck in an S shape, with its long legs trailing straight out behind. The wings are held in cupped fashion during flight. Nests in colonies of up to 100 birds. Nests in treetops near or over open water. Most common along the coast.

male

female

RUBY-THROATED HUMMINGBIRD
Archilochus colubris

SUMMER

Size:	3-3½" (7.5-9 cm)
Male:	Tiny iridescent green bird with black throat patch that reflects bright ruby red in sun.
Female:	same as male, but lacking the throat patch
Juvenile:	same as female
Nest:	cup; female builds; 1-2 broods per year
Eggs:	2; white without markings
Incubation:	12-14 days; female incubates
Fledging:	14-18 days; female feeds young
Migration:	complete, to southern states, Mexico and Central America
Food:	nectar, insects
Compare:	No other bird is as tiny. The Sphinx Moth hovers at flowers like the Hummingbird, but has clear wings and a mouth part that looks like a straw, which coils up when not at a flower. Moves much slower than the Hummingbird and can be approached.

Stan's Notes: The smallest bird in Maine. It is able to hover, fly up and down, and is the only bird to fly backward. Does not sing, but will chatter or buzz to communicate. The wings create a humming noise, flapping 50 to 60 times per second or faster during chasing flights. Weighing just 2 to 3 grams, it takes about five average-sized hummingbirds to equal the weight of a single chickadee. Its heart pumps an incredible 1,260 beats per minute, and it breathes 250 times per minute. Constructs a nest with plant material and spider webs, gluing pieces of lichen on the outside of nest for camouflage. Attracted to tubular red flowers.

male

female pg. 163

WOOD DUCK
Aix sponsa

SUMMER

Size: 17-20" (43-50 cm)

Male: A small, highly ornamented dabbling duck with a green head and crest patterned with white and black. A rusty chest, white belly and red eyes.

Female: brown, similar size and shape as male, has bright white eye-ring and a not-so-obvious crest, blue patch on wing often hidden

Juvenile: same as female

Nest: cavity; female lines old woodpecker cavity; 1 brood per year

Eggs: 10-15; creamy white without markings

Incubation: 28-36 days; female incubates

Fledging: 56-68 days; female teaches young to feed

Migration: complete, to southern states

Food: aquatic insects, plants, seeds

Compare: Male Green-winged Teal (pg. 145) is less colorful. Male Hooded Merganser (pg. 43) is similar in size, but has a crest "hood."

Stan's Notes: A common duck of quiet, shallow backwater ponds. Nearly extinct around 1900 due to overhunting, but is doing well now. Nests in an old woodpecker hole or uses a nesting box. Often seen flying deep in forest or perched high on tree branches. Female takes flight with loud squealing call and enters nest cavity from full flight. Will lay eggs in a neighboring nest (egg dumping), resulting in some clutches in excess of 20 eggs. Young remain in nest cavity 24 hours after hatching, then jump from up to 30 feet (9 m) to the ground or water to follow their mother, never returning to the nest.

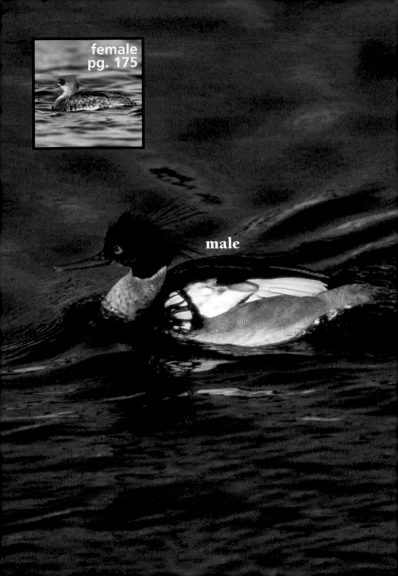

female
pg. 175

male

RED-BREASTED MERGANSER
Mergus serrator

YEAR-ROUND
MIGRATION
SUMMER
WINTER

Size: 23" (58 cm)

Male: A shaggy green head and crest. Prominent white collar. Rusty breast. Black and white body. Long orange bill.

Female: overall brown to gray with a shaggy reddish head and crest, long orange bill

Juvenile: similar to female

Nest: ground; female builds; 1 brood per year

Eggs: 5-10; olive green without markings

Incubation: 29-30 days; female incubates

Fledging: 55-65 days; female feeds young

Migration: complete, to coastal Maine and southern coastal states, Central America

Food: fish, aquatic insects

Compare: Larger than the male Hooded Merganser (pg. 43), which has a large white patch on the head, compared with the green head of the male Red-breasted Merganser.

Stan's Notes: A very fast flier, often seen flying low and fast across water. Needs a long take off run to get airborne. Serrated bill helps it catch slippery fish. Doesn't breed before 2 years of age. The male abandons female just after eggs are laid. Females often share a nest. Breeds in Alaska, northern Canada and inland Maine, wintering on the coast.

female pg. 255

male

COMMON MERGANSER
Mergus merganser

YEAR-ROUND
SUMMER

Size: 27" (69 cm)

Male: Long, thin, duck-like bird with green head, a black back, and white sides, breast and neck. Has a long, pointed orange bill. Often appears to be black and white in poor light.

Female: same size and shape as the male, but with a rust red head, ragged "hair" on head, gray body with white chest and chin, and long, pointed orange bill

Juvenile: same as female

Nest: cavity; female lines old woodpecker cavity; 1 brood per year

Eggs: 9-11; ivory without markings

Incubation: 28-33 days; female incubates

Fledging: 70-80 days; female feeds young

Migration: complete, to southern states and Mexico

Food: small fish, aquatic insects

Compare: Similar size as male Mallard (pg. 239), but male Common Merganser has a black back, bright white sides and a long pointed bill.

Stan's Notes: Mergansers are shallow water divers that feed on fish in no more than 10 to 15 feet (3 to 4.5 m) of water. The bill has a fine serrated-like edge to help catch slippery fish. Females often lay eggs in other merganser nests (egg dumping), resulting in broods of up to 15 young per mother. Male leaves female as soon as she starts to incubate eggs. Orphans are accepted by other merganser mothers with young.

female pg. 179

male

MALLARD
Anas platyrhynchos

YEAR-ROUND

Size: 27-28" (69-71 cm)

Male: Large, bulbous green head, white necklace and rust brown or chestnut chest. Gray and white on the sides. Yellow bill. Orange legs and feet.

Female: brown duck with an orange and black bill and blue and white wing mark (speculum)

Juvenile: same as female, but with a yellow bill

Nest: ground; female builds; 1 brood per year

Eggs: 7-10; greenish to whitish, unmarked

Incubation: 26-30 days; female incubates

Fledging: 42-52 days; female leads young to food

Migration: complete, to southern states, non-migrator in parts of Maine

Food: seeds, plants, aquatic insects; will come to ground feeders offering corn

Compare: Most people recognize this common duck. Larger than male Red-breasted Merganser (pg. 235), lacking the Merganser's shaggy crest and large orange bill.

Stan's Notes: A familiar duck of lakes and ponds, it's considered a type of dabbling duck, tipping forward in shallow water to feed on aquatic plants on the bottom. The name "Mallard" comes from the Latin *masculus*, meaning "male," referring to the habit of males not taking part in raising ducklings. Black central tail feathers of male curl upward. Both the male and female have white tails and white underwings. Will return to place of birth.

239

male

female pg. 273

AMERICAN REDSTART
Setophaga ruticilla

Size: 5" (13 cm)

Male: Small, striking black bird with contrasting patches of orange on sides, wings and tail. White belly.

Female: olive brown with yellow patches on sides, wings and tail, white belly

Juvenile: same as female, juvenile male attains orange tinges in the second year

Nest: cup; female builds; 1 brood per year

Eggs: 3-5; off-white with brown markings

Incubation: 12 days; female incubates

Fledging: 9 days; female and male feed young

Migration: complete, to Mexico, Central America and South America

Food: insects, seeds, berries rarely

Compare: Male Red-winged Blackbird (pg. 9) and the male Baltimore Oriole (pg. 243) are much larger at roughly 8 inches (20 cm). The only small black and orange bird flitting around tops of trees.

Stan's Notes: A common and widespread warbler in Maine that prefers large unbroken tracts of forest. Appears to be hyperactive when feeding, hovering and darting back and forth to glean insects from leaves. Frequently droops its wings and fans tail just before launching out to catch an insect. Look for the male's flashing black and orange colors high up in trees.

male

female pg. 285

BALTIMORE ORIOLE
Icterus galbula

SUMMER

Size: 7-8" (18-20 cm)

Male: Bright flaming orange bird with black head and black extending down nape of neck onto the back. Black wings with white and orange wing bars. An orange tail with black streaks. Gray bill and dark eyes.

Female: pale yellow with orange tones, gray brown wings, white wing bars, gray bill, dark eyes

Juvenile: same as female

Nest: pendulous; female builds; 1 brood per year

Eggs: 4-5; bluish with brown markings

Incubation: 12-14 days; female incubates

Fledging: 12-14 days; female and male feed young

Migration: complete, to Mexico, Central America and South America

Food: insects, fruit, nectar; comes to orange half and nectar feeders

Compare: The male American Redstart (pg. 241) is smaller and has more black than orange.

Stan's Notes: A fantastic songster, often heard before seen. Easily attracted to a feeder that offers grape jelly, orange halves or sugar water (nectar). Parents bring young to feeders. Sits in tops of trees feeding on caterpillars. Female builds a sock-like nest at outermost branches of tall trees. Often returns to the same area year after year. Some of the last birds to arrive in spring (March to April) and first to leave in fall (August).

yellow male

female pg. 83

male

HOUSE FINCH
Haemorhous mexicanus

Size: 5" (13 cm)

Male: An orange red face, breast and rump, with a brown cap. Brown marking behind eyes. Brown wings streaked with white. A white belly with brown streaks.

Female: brown with a heavily streaked white chest

Juvenile: similar to female

Nest: cup, sometimes in cavities; female builds; 2 broods per year

Eggs: 4-5; pale blue, lightly marked

Incubation: 12-14 days; female incubates

Fledging: 15-19 days; female and male feed young

Migration: non-migrator to partial migrator; will move around to find food

Food: seeds, fruit, leaf buds; will visit seed feeders

Compare: Male Purple Finch (pg. 247) is very similar, but male House Finch lacks the red crown. The male Pine Grosbeak (pg. 253) is much larger. Look for the streaked chest and belly, and brown cap of male House Finch.

Stan's Notes: Very social bird. Visits feeders in small flocks. Likes nesting in hanging flower baskets. Incubating female is fed by the male. Has a loud, cheerful warbling song. House Finches that were originally introduced to Long Island, New York, from the western U.S. in the 1940s have since populated the entire eastern U.S. Now found throughout the country. Suffers from a fatal eye disease that causes eyes to crust over. Rarely, some males are yellow (see inset) instead of red, probably due to poor diet.

female pg. 95

male

PURPLE FINCH
Haemorhous purpureus

YEAR-ROUND

Size:	6" (15 cm)
Male:	Raspberry red head, cap, breast, back and rump. Brownish wings and tail.
Female:	heavily streaked brown and white bird with large white eyebrows
Juvenile:	same as female
Nest:	cup; female and male build; 1 brood a year
Eggs:	4-5; greenish blue with brown markings
Incubation:	12-13 days; female incubates
Fledging:	13-14 days; female and male feed young
Migration:	non-migrator to irruptive; moves around in search of food
Food:	seeds, insects, fruit; comes to seed feeders
Compare:	Redder than the orange red of male House Finch (pg. 245), with a clear (no streaking) red breast. Male House Finch has a brown cap, compared with the male Purple Finch's red cap. The male Pine Grosbeak (pg. 253) is much larger.

Stan's Notes: A year-round resident throughout Maine. Common in non-residential areas (prefers open woods or woodland edges), it has been replaced in cities by House Finches. Feeds primarily on seeds, with ash tree seeds a very important food source. Will visit seed feeders along with House Finches, making it hard to tell them apart. A rich loud song, with a distinctive "tic" note made only in flight. Travels in flocks of up to 50. Not a purple color, the Latin species name *purpureus* means "purple" or other reddish colors.

female
pg. 283

male

SCARLET TANAGER
Piranga olivacea

SUMMER

Size: 7" (18 cm)

Male: Bright scarlet red bird with jet black wings and tail. Ivory bill and dark eyes.

Female: drab greenish yellow bird with olive wings and tail, whitish wing linings, dark eyes

Juvenile: same as female

Nest: cup; female builds; 1 brood per year

Eggs: 4-5; blue green with brown markings

Incubation: 13-14 days; female incubates

Fledging: 9-11 days; female and male feed young

Migration: complete, to Central and South America

Food: insects, fruit

Compare: The male Northern Cardinal (pg. 251) has black mask and red bill, and lacks the black wings of the male Scarlet Tanager.

Stan's Notes: This is a tropical-looking bird that prefers mature unbroken woodland, where it hunts for insects high in the tops of trees. Requires at least 4 acres (1.5 ha) for nesting; prefers 8 acres (3 ha). It arrives late in spring and leaves early in fall. Male sheds (molts) its bright red plumage in the fall, appearing more like the female. Scarlet Tanagers are included in some 240 tanager species in the world. Nearly all are brightly colored and live in the tropics. The common name "Tanager" comes from a South American Tupi Indian word meaning "any small, brightly colored bird."

female pg. 119

male

juvenile

NORTHERN CARDINAL
Cardinalis cardinalis

Size: 8-9" (20-22.5 cm)

Male: All-red bird with a black mask that extends from the face down to the chin and throat. Large red bill and crest.

Female: buff brown with tinges of red on crest and wings, same black mask and red bill

Juvenile: same as female, but with a blackish gray bill

Nest: cup; female builds; 2-3 broods per year

Eggs: 3-4; bluish white with brown markings

Incubation: 12-13 days; female and male incubate

Fledging: 9-10 days; female and male feed young

Migration: non-migrator

Food: seeds, insects, fruit; comes to seed feeders

Compare: Male Scarlet Tanager (pg. 249) has black wings and tail. Look for the Cardinal's black mask, large crest and red bill.

Stan's Notes: A familiar backyard bird. Look for the male feeding female during courtship. Male feeds young of the first brood by himself while female builds second nest. The name comes from the Latin word *cardinalis*, which denotes importance. Very territorial in spring, it will fight its own reflection in a window. Non-territorial during winter, gathering in small flocks of up to 20 birds. Both the male and female sing, and can be heard anytime of year. Listen for its "whata-cheer-cheer-cheer" territorial call in spring.

male

female pg. 209

PINE GROSBEAK
Pinicola enucleator

YEAR-ROUND
WINTER

Size: 9" (22.5 cm)

Male: Plump rosy red and gray winter finch with long dark tail. Dark wings have smattering of gray and two white wing bars. A short, stubby, pointed dark bill.

Female: mostly gray with dark wings and tail, head and rump tinged dull yellow

Juvenile: male has a touch of red on head and rump, female is similar to adult female

Nest: cup; female builds; 1 brood per year

Eggs: 4-5; bluish green without markings

Incubation: 13-15 days; female incubates

Fledging: 13-20 days; female and male feed young

Migration: non-migrator to irruptive; moves around to find food

Food: seeds, fruit, insects; will come to feeders

Compare: Much larger than the male Purple Finch (pg. 247) and male House Finch (pg. 245).

Stan's Notes: Very tame and approachable bird. Often seen along roads or on the ground, eating tiny grains of sand and dirt to aid digestion. A seed eater that favors coniferous woods, rarely moving out of coniferous regions during summer. Frequently seen bathing in fluffy snow. Flies with a typical finch-like undulating pattern while calling a soft whistle. During breeding season, both male and female develop a pouch in the bottom of the mouth (buccal pouch) to transport seeds to young.

male pg. 237

female

COMMON MERGANSER
Mergus merganser

YEAR-ROUND
SUMMER

Size: 27" (69 cm)

Female: A long, thin, duck-like bird with a rust red head and ragged "hair" on the back of head. Gray body with white chest and chin. Long, pointed orange bill.

Male: same size and shape as the female, but with a green head, black back, white sides and chest, and long, pointed orange bill

Juvenile: same as female

Nest: cavity; female lines old woodpecker cavity; 1 brood per year

Eggs: 9-11; ivory without markings

Incubation: 28-33 days; female incubates

Fledging: 70-80 days; female feeds young

Migration: complete, to southern states and Mexico

Food: small fish, aquatic insects

Compare: Hard to confuse with other birds. Look for ragged "hair" on back of a red head, a long, pointed orange bill, white chest and chin.

Stan's Notes: Mergansers are shallow water divers that feed on fish in no more than 10 to 15 feet (3 to 4.5 m) of water. The bill has a fine serrated-like edge to help catch slippery fish. Females often lay eggs in other merganser nests (egg dumping), resulting in broods of up to 15 young per mother. Male leaves female as soon as she starts to incubate eggs. Orphans are accepted by other merganser mothers with young.

in flight

juvenile

ARCTIC TERN
Sterna paradisaea

MIGRATION
SUMMER

Size: 12" (30 cm)

Male: White and gray tern with black crown and small dark red bill. Short red legs. Forked tail, seen in flight. Winter plumage has an incomplete black cap and black bill.

Female: same as male

Juvenile: similar to winter plumage adult, scattered brown overall

Nest: ground; the female and male build; 1 brood per year

Eggs: 2; olive with brown markings

Incubation: 20-24 days; female and male incubate

Fledging: 21-28 days; male and female feed young

Migration: complete, to South America

Food: small fish, aquatic insects, insects

Compare: Smaller than the Common Tern (pg. 259), which has a larger black-tipped bill.

Stan's Notes: Catches small fish by diving headfirst in water. Nests in large colonies with other terns such as the Common Tern. While most nesting occurs in Canada's Northwest Territories and Alaska, will nest as far south as Maine. Returns to same nest site every year. Vigorously defends nest site and young from predators and people. Long-term relationship between mates. Young stay with the adults during migration to South America.

in flight

COMMON TERN
Sterna hirundo

MIGRATION
SUMMER

Size: 13-16" (33-40 cm)

Male: White and gray tern with a jet black crown. Red-orange bill with black tip. Long white forked "tern" tail. Feet and legs red. Tips of wings dark gray when seen in flight.

Female: same as male

Juvenile: similar to adult, with a blue-gray back and white-streaked chest and neck, incomplete brown-to-black cap

Nest: ground; the female and male build; 1 brood per year

Eggs: 1-3; olive brown with brown markings

Incubation: 21-27 days; female and male incubate

Fledging: 26-27 days; female and male feed young

Migration: complete, to South America

Food: fish, aquatic insects

Compare: Very similar to Arctic Tern (pg. 257), but the Common Tern is larger in size and has a larger bill with a black tip.

Stan's Notes: This tern was nearly eliminated from the state prior to 1900 due to plume hunting. Protected by 1910, it has made a comeback. Arrives during April at nesting grounds, often on small islands. Nests in large colonies. Often associated with Arctic Terns. Competition and predation from gulls and birds of prey keep the population from expanding.

winter

breeding

LAUGHING GULL
Leucophaeus atricilla

SUMMER

Size: 16-17" (40-43 cm); up to 3⅓-foot wingspan

Male: Breeding adult has a black head "hood" and white neck, chest and belly. Slate gray back and wings with black wing tips. Orange bill. Winter plumage lacks the "hood" and has a black bill.

Female: same as male

Juvenile: brown throughout, gray sides, lacking the black head and white chest, has a gray bill

Nest: ground; the male and female build; 1 brood per year

Eggs: 2-4; olive with brown markings

Incubation: 18-20 days; female and male incubate

Fledging: 30-35 days; male and female feed young

Migration: complete, to East and Gulf coasts, Mexico, Central and South America

Food: fish, insects, aquatic insects

Compare: Smaller than the Ring-billed Gull (pg. 263) and Herring Gull (pg. 265). Look for black head "hood" and slate gray back and wings of Laughing Gull.

Stan's Notes: This is a three-year gull that starts out mostly brown and gray. The second year it resembles adults, but lacks a complete black head "hood." Breeding plumage in the third year. Male tosses its head back and calls to attract a mate. Nests in marshes in large colonies. Nest is a scrape on the ground lined with grass, sticks and rocks. Adults feed young a half-digested regurgitant.

winter

juvenile

breeding

RING-BILLED GULL
Larus delawarensis

YEAR-ROUND
MIGRATION
SUMMER

Size: 19" (48 cm); up to 4-foot wingspan

Male: A white bird with gray wings, black wing tips spotted with white, and a white tail, as seen in flight. Yellow bill with a black ring near tip. Yellowish legs and feet. Winter or non-breeding adult has a speckled brown back of head and nape of neck.

Female: same as male

Juvenile: brown speckles, a mostly dark bill, brown tip of tail

Nest: ground; the female and male build; 1 brood per year

Eggs: 2-4; off-white with brown markings

Incubation: 20-21 days; female and male incubate

Fledging: 20-40 days; female and male feed young

Migration: complete, to coastal Maine and southern coastal states, Mexico

Food: insects, fish; scavenges for food

Compare: Similar to Herring Gull (pg. 265), which has an orange mark on tip of lower bill. Herring Gull has pink legs and feet, and lacks Ring-billed's black ring.

Stan's Notes: A common gull of garbage dumps and parking lots. One of the few gulls that winters in Maine, it is expanding its range and remaining farther north longer in the winter due to successful scavenging in cities. A three-year gull with a new, different plumage in each of the first three autumns. Attains ring on bill after its first winter. Doesn't attain adult plumage until the third year.

breeding

winter

HERRING GULL
Larus argentatus

Size: 23-26" (58-66 cm); up to 5-foot wingspan

Male: Snow-white bird with slate gray wings and black wing tips with tiny white spots. Bill is yellow with an orange-red spot near tip of the lower bill. Pinkish legs. Winter plumage has gray speckles on head and neck.

Female: same as male

Juvenile: uniformly mottled brown to gray, black bill

Nest: ground; the female and male build; 1 brood per year

Eggs: 2-3; olive with brown markings

Incubation: 24-28 days; female and male incubate

Fledging: 35-36 days; female and male feed young

Migration: complete, to coasts that remain unfrozen in North America, non-migrator in Maine

Food: fish, insects, clams, eggs, baby birds

Compare: Larger than the Ring-billed Gull (pg. 263), which has yellowish legs and a black ring around its bill, and lacks an orange-red dot on the lower mandible.

YEAR-ROUND
MIGRATION
SUMMER

Stan's Notes: Common gull of large lakes. An opportunistic bird, scavenging for food from dumpsters, but will also take other birds' eggs and young right from nest. Often drops clams and other shellfish from heights to break shells and get to the soft interior. Nests in colonies, returning to same site year after year. Lines ground nest with grasses and seaweed. Takes about four years for juveniles to obtain adult plumage. Adults have spotted heads during winter.

GREAT EGRET
Ardea alba

MIGRATION
SUMMER

Size: 38" (96 cm)

Male: Tall, thin, elegant all-white bird with long, pointed yellow bill. Black stilt-like legs and black feet.

Female: same as male

Juvenile: same as adult

Nest: platform; male and female build; 1 brood per year

Eggs: 2-3; light blue without markings

Incubation: 23-26 days; female and male incubate

Fledging: 43-49 days; female and male feed young

Migration: complete, to southern coastal states, Mexico and Central America

Food: fish, aquatic insects, frogs, crayfish

Compare: Smaller in size than the Great Blue Heron (pg. 229), but similar in shape.

Stan's Notes: A tall and stately bird, the Great Egret slowly stalks shallow wetlands looking for small fish to spear with its long sharp bill. Nests in colonies of up to 100 birds. Now protected, they were hunted to near extinction in the 1800s and early 1900s for their long white plumage. The name "Egret" came from the French word *aigrette*, which means "ornamental tufts of plumes." The plumes grow near the tail during breeding season.

male

winter male

female

AMERICAN GOLDFINCH
Spinus tristis

YEAR-ROUND

Size: 5" (13 cm)

Male: A perky yellow bird with a black patch on forehead. Black tail with conspicuous white rump. Black wings with white wing bars. No marking on the chest. Dramatic change in color during winter, similar to female.

Female: dull olive yellow without a black forehead, with brown wings and white rump

Juvenile: same as female

Nest: cup; female builds; 1 brood per year

Eggs: 4-6; pale blue without markings

Incubation: 10-12 days; female incubates

Fledging: 11-17 days; female and male feed young

Migration: partial migrator to non-migrator; flocks of up to 20 birds move around North America

Food: seeds, insects; will come to seed feeders

Compare: Male Yellow Warbler (pg. 275) is all yellow with orange streaking on chest. Pine Siskin (pg. 81) has a streaked chest and belly, with yellow wing bars. The female House Finch (pg. 83) and female Purple Finch (pg. 95) both have heavily streaked chests.

Stan's Notes: Year-round resident most often found in open fields, scrubby areas and woodlands. Often called Wild Canary. A feeder bird that enjoys Nyjer seed. Late summer nesting, uses the silky down from wild thistle for nest. Appears roller-coaster-like during flight. Listen for it to twitter in flight. Almost always in small flocks. Moves only far enough south to find food.

COMMON YELLOWTHROAT
Geothlypis trichas

SUMMER

Size: 5" (13 cm)

Male: Olive brown bird with bright yellow throat and breast, a white belly and a distinctive black mask outlined in white. A long, thin, pointed black bill.

Female: same as male, but lacking the black mask

Juvenile: same as female

Nest: cup; female builds; 2 broods per year

Eggs: 3-5; white with brown markings

Incubation: 11-12 days; female incubates

Fledging: 10-11 days; female and male feed young

Migration: complete, to southern states, Mexico and Central America

Food: insects

Compare: Found in a similar habitat as the American Goldfinch (pg. 269), but lacks the male's black forehead and wings. The male Yellow Warbler (pg. 275) has fine orange streaks on chest and lacks the black mask. Yellow-rumped Warbler (pg. 193) has only spots of yellow, compared with the Yellowthroat's yellow breast.

Stan's Notes: A common warbler of open fields and marshes. Has a cheerful, well-known song, "witchity-witchity-witchity-witchity." The male performs a curious courtship display, bouncing in and out of tall grass while uttering an unusual song. The young remain dependent upon the parents longer than most warblers. A frequent cowbird host.

male pg. 241

female

AMERICAN REDSTART
Setophaga ruticilla

SUMMER

Size: 5" (13 cm)

Female: Olive brown with yellow patches on sides, wings and tail. White belly.

Male: small, striking black bird with contrasting patches of orange on sides, wings and tail, white belly

Juvenile: same as female, juvenile male attains orange tinges in the second year

Nest: cup; female builds; 1 brood per year

Eggs: 3-5; off-white with brown markings

Incubation: 12 days; female incubates

Fledging: 9 days; female and male feed young

Migration: complete, to Mexico, Central America and South America

Food: insects, seeds, berries rarely

Compare: Similar to female Yellow-rumped Warbler (pg. 193), but lacking the Warbler's yellow patch on rump.

Stan's Notes: A common and widespread warbler in Maine that prefers large unbroken tracts of forest. Appears to be hyperactive when feeding, hovering and darting back and forth to glean insects from leaves. Frequently droops its wings and fans tail just before launching out to catch an insect. Look for the male's flashing black and orange colors high up in trees.

YELLOW WARBLER
Setophaga petechia

Size: 5" (13 cm)

Male: Yellow warbler with orange streaks on the chest and belly. Long, pointed dark bill.

Female: same as male, but lacking orange streaking

Juvenile: similar to female, only much duller

Nest: cup; female builds; 1 brood per year

Eggs: 4-5; white with brown markings

Incubation: 11-12 days; female incubates

Fledging: 10-12 days; female and male feed young

Migration: complete, to southern states, Mexico, and Central and South America

Food: insects

Compare: Yellow-rumped Warbler (pg. 193) has only spots of yellow, compared with the orange streaking on chest of male Yellow Warbler. Male American Goldfinch (pg. 269) has black wings and forehead. Female Warbler is similar to the female American Goldfinch (pg. 269), but lacks the white wing bars.

Stan's Notes: A scattered but widespread warbler in Maine. Seen in gardens and shrubby areas close to water. A prolific insect eater, gleaning small caterpillars and other insects from tree leaves. The male is often seen higher up in trees than the female. Female is less conspicuous. Seen during migration beginning in August, when birds north of Maine move through the state. Returns in April. The males arrive a week or two before the females to claim territories. Migrates at night in mixed flocks of warblers. Rests and feeds days

male

female

MAGNOLIA WARBLER
Setophaga magnolia

SUMMER

Size: 5" (13 cm)

Male: Yellow and black warbler with a gray crown and white eyebrows. Heavy black streaks on a yellow chest and belly. White wing patch. Yellow rump. Obvious white patches on tail.

Female: similar to male, lacks black on face, has two white wing bars

Juvenile: same as female

Nest: cup; female and male build; 1 brood a year

Eggs: 3-5; white with brown markings

Incubation: 11-13 days; female incubates

Fledging: 8-10 days; female and male feed young

Migration: complete, to Central America

Food: insects

Compare: More yellow than Yellow-rumped Warbler (pg. 193). The Yellow Warbler (pg. 275) lacks a black face and back. Palm Warbler (pg. 279) has a chestnut crown and thin chestnut streaks on sides of breast.

Stan's Notes: A common and widespread warbler in Maine. Can be more abundant during migration, when groups move together. Look for it low in trees, where it feeds on insects. Frequently fans its tail while picking insects from undersides of leaves. Male often feeds higher up in trees than female. Nests throughout Maine and Canada. Named by chance when ornithologist Alexander Wilson spotted the bird in a magnolia tree.

PALM WARBLER
Setophaga palmarum

MIGRATION
SUMMER

Size: 5½" (14 cm)

Male: Distinctive yellow eyebrows. Yellow throat, belly and undertail. An obvious chestnut-colored crown. On the sides of breast, thin chestnut-colored streaks. A dark line across dark eyes.

Female: same as male

Juvenile: same as adult, but duller and brown

Nest: cup; female builds; 1-2 broods per year

Eggs: 4-5; white with brown markings

Incubation: 11-12 days; female incubates

Fledging: 12-13 days; female and male feed young

Migration: complete, to southeastern coastal states, the West Indies and Central America

Food: insects, fruit

Compare: Similar size as the Yellow-rumped Warbler (pg. 193), but Yellow-rumped lacks yellow throat and belly. Pine Warbler (pg. 281) has pronounced white wing bars. Look for the yellow eyebrows and chestnut cap.

Stan's Notes: A common and widespread breeding warbler in the state. Can be more numerous during migration, when birds north of Maine pass through the state. Look for it to wag or bob its tail while gleaning insects from leaves and flowers of trees. One of the few warblers to feed on the ground. Hops rather than walks. Nests at edges of northern spruce bogs. Recognizes and destroys cowbird eggs, burying them with its nest, which it builds over the top of the cowbird nest.

PINE WARBLER
Setophaga pinus

Size: 5½" (14 cm)

Male: A yellow throat and breast with faint black streaks on sides of breast. Olive green back. Two white wing bars. White belly.

Female: similar to male, only paler

Juvenile: similar to adults, only browner, more white on belly

Nest: cup; female builds; 2-3 broods per year

Eggs: 3-5; white with brown markings

Incubation: 10-12 days; female incubates

Fledging: 12-14 days; female and male feed young

Migration: complete, to southern states

Food: insects, seeds, fruit

Compare: Similar to Palm Warbler (pg. 279), lacking the brown cap and yellow eyebrows of the Palm. The Pine Warbler has much more pronounced white wing bars than the Palm.

Stan's Notes: A common resident of pine forests in the southern two-thirds of the state. Builds nest only in pine forest. Brighter in spring and more drab in autumn, it varies in color depending on the time of year. Thought to have a larger bill than other warblers. Sometimes it is easier to identify by song than sight. Listen for a twittering, musical song that varies in speed.

female

male pg. 249

SCARLET TANAGER
Piranga olivacea

SUMMER

Size: 7" (18 cm)

Female: Drab greenish yellow bird with olive wings and tail. Whitish wing linings. Dark eyes.

Male: bright scarlet red bird with jet black wings and tail, ivory bill and dark eyes

Juvenile: same as female

Nest: cup; female builds; 1 brood per year

Eggs: 4-5; blue green with brown markings

Incubation: 13-14 days; female incubates

Fledging: 9-11 days; female and male feed young

Migration: complete, to Central and South America

Food: insects, fruit

Compare: Female Northern Cardinal (pg. 119) has black mask and red bill, but lacks the dark wings of the female Scarlet Tanager. Larger than female American Goldfinch (pg. 269) and lacks the Goldfinch's white wing bars. Female Baltimore Oriole (pg. 285) has gray brown wings and white wing bars.

Stan's Notes: This is a tropical-looking bird that prefers mature unbroken woodland, where it hunts for insects high in the tops of trees. Requires at least 4 acres (1.5 ha) for nesting; prefers 8 acres (3 ha). It arrives late in spring and leaves early in fall. Male sheds (molts) its bright red plumage in the fall, appearing more like the female. Scarlet Tanagers are included in some 240 tanager species in the world. Nearly all are brightly colored and live in the tropics. The common name "Tanager" comes from a South American Tupi Indian word meaning "any small, brightly colored bird."

male pg. 243

female

BALTIMORE ORIOLE
Icterus galbula

SUMMER

Size: 7-8" (18-20 cm)

Female: A pale yellow bird with orange tones, gray brown wings, white wing bars, a gray bill and dark eyes.

Male: bright flaming orange bird with black head and black extending down nape of neck onto the back, black wings with white and orange wing bars, an orange tail with black streaks, gray bill and dark eyes

Juvenile: same as female

Nest: pendulous; female builds; 1 brood per year

Eggs: 4-5; bluish with brown markings

Incubation: 12-14 days; female incubates

Fledging: 12-14 days; female and male feed young

Migration: complete, to Mexico, Central America and South America

Food: insects, fruit, nectar; comes to orange half and nectar feeders

Compare: Female Baltimore Oriole is often confused with the female Scarlet Tanager (pg. 283), which has olive-colored wings.

Stan's Notes: A fantastic songster, often heard before seen. Easily attracted to a feeder that offers grape jelly, orange halves or sugar water (nectar). Parents bring young to feeders. Sits in tops of trees feeding on caterpillars. Female builds a sock-like nest at outermost branches of tall trees. Often returns to the same area year after year. Some of the last birds to arrive in spring (March to April) and first to leave in fall (August).

YEAR-ROUND

EVENING GROSBEAK
Coccothraustes vespertinus

Size: 8" (20 cm)

Male: A striking bird with a stocky body, a large ivory-to-greenish bill and bright yellow eyebrows. Dirty yellow head, black-and-white wings and tail, and yellow rump and belly.

Female: similar to male, with softer colors, and gray head and throat

Juvenile: same as female, but with a brown bill

Nest: cup; female builds; 1 brood per year

Eggs: 3-4; blue with brown markings

Incubation: 12-14 days; female incubates

Fledging: 13-14 days; female and male feed young

Migration: irruptive; moves around the state in search of food

Food: seeds, insects, fruit; comes to seed feeders

Compare: Larger than its close relative, the American Goldfinch (pg. 269). Look for the dark head with bright yellow eyebrows and the extra-large bill.

Stan's Notes: One of the largest finches. Characteristic undulating finch-like flight. An unusually large bill for cracking seeds, its main food source. Often seen on gravel roads eating gravel, from which it gets minerals, salt and grit to grind the seeds it eats. A year-round resident, it is more obvious during winter because it moves in large flocks, searching for food, often coming to feeders. Sheds the outer layer of its bill in spring, exposing a blue green bill.

EASTERN MEADOWLARK
Sturnella magna

SUMMER

Size: 9" (22.5 cm)

Male: Robin-shaped bird with brown back, yellow chest and belly, and a prominent black V-shaped necklace. White outer tail feathers.

Female: same as male

Juvenile: same as adult

Nest: cup, on the ground in dense cover; female builds; 2 broods per year

Eggs: 3-5; white with brown markings

Incubation: 13-15 days; female incubates

Fledging: 11-12 days; female and male feed young

Migration: complete, to southern states, Mexico and Central America

Food: insects, seeds

Compare: The only large yellow bird with a black V mark on chest.

Stan's Notes: A bird of open grassy country. Named "Meadowlark" because it's a bird of meadows and sings like the larks of Europe. Best known for its wonderful song–a flute-like, clear whistle. Often seen perching on fence posts, it will quickly dive into tall grass if approached. Conspicuous white markings on each side of its tail, most often seen when flying away. Nest is sometimes domed with dried grass. Not a member of the lark family, it actually belongs to the blackbird family. Related to grackles and orioles.

Helpful Resources:

Birder's Bug Book, The. Waldbauer, Gilbert. Cambridge: Harvard University Press, 1998.

Birder's Dictionary. Cox, Randall T. Helena, MT: Falcon Press Publishing, 1996.

Birder's Guide to Maine, A. Pierson, Elizabeth C., Jan E. Pierson and Peter D. Vickery. Camden, ME: Down East Books, 1996.

Birder's Handbook, The. Ehrlich, Paul R., David S. Dobkin and Darryl Wheye. New York: Simon and Schuster, 1988.

Birds Do It, Too: The Amazing Sex Life of Birds. Harrison, Kit and George H. Harrison. Minocqua, WI: Willow Creek Press, 1997.

Birds of Forest, Yard, and Thicket. Eastman, John. Mechanicsburg, PA: Stackpole Books, 1997.

Birds of North America. Kaufman, Kenn. New York: Houghton Mifflin, 2000.

Blackbirds of the Americas. Orians, Gordon H. Seattle: University of Washington Press, 1985.

Cardinal, The. Osborne, June. Austin: University of Texas Press, 1995.

Dictionary of American Bird Names, The. Choate, Ernest A. Boston: Harvard Common Press, 1985.

Everything You Never Learned About Birds. Rupp, Rebecca. Pownal, VT: Storey Publishing, 1997.

Field Guide to the Birds, A: A Completely New Guide to All the Birds of Eastern and Central North America. Peterson, Roger Tory and Virginia Marie Peterson. Boston: Houghton Mifflin, 1998.

Field Guide to the Birds of North America: Third Edition. Washington, D.C.: National Geographic Society, 1999.

Field Guide to Warblers of North America, A. Dunn, Jon and Kimball Garrett. Boston: Houghton Mifflin, 1997.

Folklore of Birds. Martin, Laura C. Old Saybrook, CT: Globe Pequot Press, 1996.

Guide to Bird Behavior, A: Vol I, II, III. Stokes, Donald and Lillian Stokes. Boston: Little, Brown and Company, 1989.

How Birds Migrate. Kerlinger, Paul. Mechanicsburg, PA: Stackpole Books, 1995.

Lives of Birds, The: Birds of the World and Their Behavior. Short, Lester L. Collingdale, PA: DIANE Publishing, 2000.

Lives of North American Birds. Kaufman, Kenn. Boston: Houghton Mifflin, 1996.

Living on the Wind. Weidensaul, Scott. New York: North Point Press, 2000.

National Audubon Society: North American Birdfeeder Handbook. Burton, Robert. New York: Dorling Kindersley Publishing, 1995.

National Audubon Society: The Sibley Guide to Bird Life and Behavior. Edited by David Allen Sibley, Chris Elphick and John B. Dunning, Jr. New York: Alfred A. Knopf, 2001.

National Audubon Society: The Sibley Guide to Birds. Sibley, David Allen. New York: Alfred A. Knopf, 2000.

Photographic Guide to North American Raptors, A. Wheeler, Brian K. and William S. Clark. New York: Academic Press, 1999.

Secret Lives of Birds, The. Gingras, Pierre. Toronto: Key Porter Books, 1997.

Secrets of the Nest. Dunning, Joan. Boston: Houghton Mifflin, 1994.

Sparrows and Buntings: A Guide to the Sparrows and Buntings of North America and the World. Byers, Clive, Jon Curson and Urban Olsson. New York: Houghton Mifflin, 1995.

Stokes Bluebird Book: The Complete Guide to Attracting Bluebirds. Stokes, Donald and Lillian Stokes. Boston: Little, Brown and Company, 1991.

Stokes Field Guide to Birds: Eastern Region. Stokes, Donald and Lillian Stokes. Boston: Little, Brown and Company, 1996.

Stokes Purple Martin Book. Stokes, Donald and Lillian Stokes. Boston: Little, Brown and Company, 1997.

MAINE BIRDING HOTLINES:

To report unusual bird sightings or possibly hear recordings of where birds have been seen, you can often call pre-recorded hotlines detailing such information. Since these hotlines are usually staffed by volunteers, and phone numbers and even the organizations that host them often change, the phone numbers are not listed here. To obtain the numbers, go to your favorite internet search engine, type in something like "rare bird alert hotline Maine" and follow the links provided.

WEB PAGES:

The internet is a valuable place to learn more about birds. You may find birding on the net a fun way to discover additional information or to spend a long winter night. These websites will assist you in your pursuit of birds. If a web address doesn't work (they often change a bit), just enter the name of the group into a search engine to track down the new address.

SITE	ADDRESS
Maine Audubon	www.maineaudubon.org
American Birding Association	www.aba.org
Cornell Lab of Ornithology	www.birds.cornell.edu
Author Stan Tekiela's home page	www.naturesmart.com

CHECKLIST/INDEX

Use the boxes to check the birds you've seen.

ABOUT THE AUTHOR:

Naturalist, wildlife photographer and writer Stan Tekiela is the originator of the popular state-specific field guide series that includes *Birds of Massachusetts Field Guide*. Stan has authored more than 190 educational books, including field guides, quick guides, nature books, children's books, playing cards and more, presenting many species of animals and plants.

With a Bachelor of Science degree in Natural History from the University of Minnesota and as an active professional naturalist for more than 30 years, Stan studies and photographs wildlife throughout the United States and Canada. He has received various national and regional awards for his books and photographs. Also a well-known columnist and radio personality, his syndicated column appears in more than 25 newspapers, and his wildlife programs are broadcast on a number of Midwest radio stations. Stan can be followed on Facebook and Twitter. He can be contacted via www.naturesmart.com.